MASTERING BASIC SKILLS
KINDERGARTEN

Brighter Child®
An imprint of Carson Dellosa Education
Greensboro, North Carolina

Brighter Child®
An imprint of Carson Dellosa Education
P.O. Box 35665
Greensboro, NC 27425-5665

carsondellosa.com

Printed in the USA. All rights reserved.
ISBN 978-1-4838-0105-6

14-031221151

Table of Contents

Table of Contents

Contents by Skill

Contents by Skill

Introduction

Welcome to *Mastering Basic Skills*. Kindergarten is an exciting and rewarding time for young children. In kindergarten, the foundation is being built for academic success. Children are discovering that learning is fun, which makes them want to achieve.

Energetic kindergartners need a great deal of guidance, have short attention spans, and are generally helpful, but they can also demonstrate extremes in behavior. Five-year-olds can be like the traditional rhyme of the little girl with the curl in the middle of her forehead—when five- and six-year-olds are good, they are very good, but when they fall apart, it can be difficult. The lesson is to be patient—children learn so much and so fast!

Kindergartners are rapid learners. As you look through the activities in this book, please keep in mind that all children mature and develop skills at different rates. Some kindergartners love pencil and paper tasks, while others would rather learn through building, putting together puzzles, or with pretend and movement activities. You will grow with your child and begin to discover many of the ways that your child learns best. Be creative and adjust each task to meet the needs of your child.

Remember that young kindergartners are not only learning academic skills, but they are also learning how to participate in groups and express their feelings. Their self-esteem is increasing, and they are beginning to understand their own uniqueness. The activities in this book were designed for you and your child to complete together. Your kindergartner needs your support, your guidance, your participation, and your undivided attention. You are the one who will help set the stage for future school success!

Everyday Ways to Enrich Learning Experiences

Language Arts

The single most important skill that a child needs for success in school, and later in life, is to be "literate." In other words, your child must learn how to read. You can do many things to encourage literacy.

- Read to your child every day and ask your child questions about key details in the text, such as identifying the major characters, settings, and events in the story.
- Talk about the pictures.
- Ask your child to guess what is going to happen next.
- Encourage your child to retell favorite stories or favorite parts of a story.
- Have your child make up a new ending for a story.
- Ask your child to compare and contrast the experiences of two different characters in familiar stories.
- Go to the library and let your child choose new books.
- Encourage "pretend" reading. This is when children look at the pictures and make up what they think the words say.
- Have your child write a text that explains how to do something he or she loves using a combination of drawing, dictating, and writing.
- Point out letters in the environment, such as on cereal boxes, in your child's name, and on billboards.
- With guidance, help your child explore digital tools for writing, such as typing letters on a computer or gathering information from the Internet.
- Find ways to help your child learn to match letters.
- Play listening games. Have your child identify words that begin with the same sound.
- Play rhyming word games and make up silly poems together.
- Identify common sight words in the environment, such as "stop."
- Fill your child's environment with literacy materials like magnetic letters, books, magazines, newspapers, catalogs, paper, pencils, crayons, paints, and CDs of children's music or recorded children's stories.
- Encourage your child to draw or write thank-you notes or letters.
- Together, make a scrapbook of kindergarten memories.

Math & Science

So many toys and puzzles provide young children with early math and science learning experiences. Remember to point out all the ways we use numbers and science in our daily lives. Here are some suggested activities:

- Give your child a magnifying glass to explore his or her environment.
- Provide lots of blocks and other building materials in a variety of geometric shapes. Have your child build things in two different ways.
- Draw shapes (squares, circles, triangles, rectangles, hexagons, cubes, cones, cylinders, and spheres) on paper and ask your child to identify the shapes as two-dimensional ("flat") or three-dimensional ("solid").
- Give your child magnetic numerals. Allow your child to put the numbers in the correct sequence or identify missing numbers in the number sequence.
- Use scales to measure objects around your house to teach the concepts of heavier and lighter. Use rulers to compare lengths and heights of different objects.
- Give your child a variety of objects to classify and sort in different ways. For instance, have your child sort socks by color then he or she can sort them by size.
- Use objects such as beads or pennies to decompose numbers 11–19 into ten ones and some further ones. For instance, use a group of ten beads and four beads to visualize the number 14.
- Sink and float objects during bath time. Have your child categorize objects that sink and float and observe similarities, such as heavier objects sink and lighter objects float.
- Provide your child with a variety of puzzles.
- Play hide and seek where your child must count out loud to 100 by ones before finding you. Then, play a fast-paced round where your child counts out loud to 100 by tens.
- Take trips to science and children's museums. Ask your child to tell you what he or she learned.
- Take walks and make observations about nature and patterns in nature.
- Make up pretend story problems during everyday activities, like snack time. Help your child solve the problems using visual aids.

Recommended Books for Kindergartners

A

ABC, I Like Me! by Nancy Carlson
The Accidental Zucchini: An Unexpected Alphabet by Max Grover
Airplanes by Byron Barton
Alicia Has a Bad Day by Lisa Jahn-Clough
Alphababies by Kim Golding
Arf! Beg! Catch! Dogs from A to Z by Henry Horenstein
Arthur's Family Vacation by Marc Brown
Arthur's First Sleepover by Marc Brown
Arthur's Neighborhood by Marc Brown
Arthur's Teacher Trouble by Marc Brown

B

Bats by Gail Gibbons
Bear in a Square by Stella Blackstone
Bearsie Bear and the Surprise Sleepover Party by Bernard Waber
Big Anthony and the Magic Ring by Tomie dePaola
Boats by Byron Barton
Brown Bear, Brown Bear, What Do You See? by Bill Martin Jr.

C

Cats by Gail Gibbons
Cinderella by Alan Trussell-Cullen
Clifford Gets a Job by Norman Bridwell
Clifford, the Big Red Dog by Norman Bridwell
Clifford's ABC by Norman Bridwell
Clifford's Good Deeds by Norman Bridwell
Clifford's Puppy Days by Norman Bridwell
Color Dance by Ann Jonas
Corduroy's Christmas by B. G. Hennessy
The Crayon Counting Book by Pam Muñoz Ryan and Jerry Pallotta

D

Do You Want to Be My Friend? by Eric Carle
The Doorbell Rang by Pat Hutchins

E

Eating the Alphabet by Lois Ehlert

F

Five Little Monkeys Jumping on the Bed by Eileen Christelow
Flossie and the Fox by Patricia C. McKissack
Franklin and the Thunderstorm by Paulette Bourgeois
Franklin Goes to School by Paulette Bourgeois
Franklin in the Dark by Paulette Bourgeois
Franklin Is Bossy by Paulette Bourgeois
Franklin Is Lost by Paulette Bourgeois
Franklin's New Friend by Paulette Bourgeois
The Frog Prince by Alan Trussell-Cullen

G

The Gingerbread Boy by Paul Galdone
Golden Bear by Ruth Young
The Grouchy Ladybug by Eric Carle
Growing Vegetable Soup by Lois Ehlert

H

Harold and the Purple Crayon by Crockett Johnson

I

I Know an Old Lady Who Swallowed a Fly, retold and illustrated by Nadine Bernard Westcott
I Went Walking by Sue Williams
If You Give a Moose a Muffin by Laura Joffe Numeroff
If You Give a Mouse a Cookie by Laura Joffe Numeroff
Ira Sleeps Over by Bernard Waber
The Island Light by Rosemary Wells
It's a Fruit, It's a Vegetable, It's a Pumpkin by Allan Fowler

J

Julius, the Baby of the World by Kevin Henkes

K

K Is for Kiss Good Night: A Bedtime Alphabet by Jill Sardegna

L

Lilly's Purple Plastic Purse by Kevin Henkes
Louie's Goose by H. M. Ehrlich

M

Make Way for Ducklings by Robert McCloskey
Meow! retold and illustrated by Katya Arnold
Mike Mulligan and His Steam Shovel
    by Virginia Lee Burton
Miss Bindergarten Gets Ready for
    Kindergarten by Joseph Slate
Miss Spider's Tea Party by David Kirk
The Mitten: A Ukrainian Folktale, adapted and
    illustrated by Jan Brett
The Mixed-Up Chameleon by Eric Carle
Monkey-Monkey's Trick: Based on an African
    Folktale by Patricia C. McKissack
Moss Pillows by Rosemary Wells
Mouse Mess by Linnea Riley
My Friend Gorilla by Atsuko Morozumi
My Little Sister Ate One Hare by Bill Grossman

O

Our Granny by Margaret Wild
Over in the Meadow by John Langstaff

P

Pigs by Gail Gibbons
The Polar Express by Chris Van Allsburg
The Princess and the Pea
    by Alan Trussell-Cullen
Pumpkin, Pumpkin by Jeanne Titherington
Purple, Green, and Yellow by Robert Munsch

Q

The Quilt Story by Tony Johnston

R

Rabbits, Rabbits, and More Rabbits!
    by Gail Gibbons
The Rainbow Fish by Marcus Pfister
The Relatives Came by Cynthia Rylant
Rooster's Off to See the World by Eric Carle

S

Silver Packages: An Appalachian Christmas
    Story by Cynthia Rylant

Skip to My Lou, adapted and illustrated by
    Nadine Bernard Westcott
Stellaluna by Janell Cannon
Strega Nona: An Old Tale, retold and
    illustrated by Tomie de Paola
Strega Nona's Magic Lessons
    by Tomie de Paola
The Story of Ruby Bridges by Robert Coles
A Summertime Song by Irene Haas

T

To Market, to Market by Anne Miranda
Thank You, Santa by Margaret Wild
This Old Man, illustrated by Carol Jones
The Three Little Pigs, illustrated by Eileen Grace
Tom Goes to Kindergarten by Margaret Wild
The Town Mouse and the Country Mouse,
    retold and illustrated by Helen Craig
Trucks by Byron Barton
Trucks You Can Count On by Doug Magee
Tucking Mommy In by Morag Loh

V

The Very Busy Spider by Eric Carle
The Very Clumsy Click Beetle by Eric Carle
The Very Hungry Caterpillar by Eric Carle
The Very Quiet Cricket by Eric Carle
Voyage to the Bunny Planet: First Tomato
    by Rosemary Wells

W

What Will Mommy Do When I'm at School?
    by Dolores Johnson
When I Feel Angry by Cornelia Maude
    Spelman
Where's Spot? by Eric Hill
White Rabbit's Color Book by Alan Baker
The Wimp by Kathy Caple

Z

Zoo-Looking by Mem Fox

★ Any book by Dr. Seuss

My Parents and Me: Cooking Fun

Easy Banana Ice Cream

Making ice cream on a hot summer day is always a treat for a young child. Here is an easy (and unique) ice cream recipe.

You will need: ½ cup orange juice, 3 ripe bananas, 12 marshmallows, 1 tablespoon sugar, a dash of salt, yellow food coloring (optional), 1 cup whipping cream, measuring spoons, 2 mixing bowls, a hand mixer, a knife, an 8" round cake pan, foil, and a stirring spoon.

Directions: Assist your child in cutting the bananas into large chunks. In a large mixing bowl, combine all the ingredients except the whipping cream. Using the hand mixer, blend at high speed for one minute. In a separate bowl, mix the whipping cream until peaks form. Fold the whipped cream into the banana mixture. Pour into a cake pan, cover with foil, and freeze until firm.

Apple Cinnamon Toast

Sometimes it is difficult to get a child to eat a good breakfast. Here is a fun idea that your little one is sure to enjoy.

You will need: 1 apple, cinnamon-sugar mixture in a shaker, 1 slice of bread, butter, a knife, and a cookie sheet.

Directions: Peel and slice the apple. Let your child butter the bread and place the apple slices on the bread. Shake the cinnamon-sugar mixture over the top. Place on a cookie sheet and bake at 375°F for 15 to 20 minutes. Not only is this good for breakfast, but it also makes a great snack!

Pretzels

This recipe is lots of fun and provides a healthy, great-tasting treat for your child. Any extra pretzels can be frozen and saved for another day.

You will need: 1 package yeast, 1½ cups warm water, 1 tablespoon sugar, 4 cups flour, 1 egg (beaten), salt, a mixing bowl, a basting brush, measuring cups, measuring spoons, and a cookie sheet.

Directions: In a mixing bowl, dissolve the yeast in the warm water. Add the flour and sugar. Knead the mixture on a floured board or table-top. (Kids are great at kneading bread.) Let the dough rise until it doubles in size. Divide the dough in half, then in half again. Split each quarter into three pieces. Take each piece and roll out into a long tube. Twist the tube into the shape of a pretzel. Brush with egg and sprinkle with salt. Bake at 450°F for 15 minutes. Makes 12 large pretzels.

Finger Gelatin

It is so much fun to eat gelatin with your fingers!

You will need: 2 envelopes unflavored gelatin and 2 packages Jell-O brand gelatin.

Directions: Follow the directions on the Jell-O package, adding the two envelopes of unflavored gelatin, too. Pour into a pan and chill until firm. Cut with a knife, or create shapes with cookie cutters.

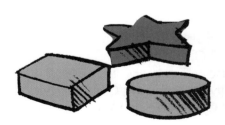

Create Your Own Puppets

Let's start vacation time with something silly. Here is a page of eyes, noses, mouths, and ears for creating some really silly puppets. Color and cut out the pieces. Glue them onto the bottom of a lunch-size paper bag.

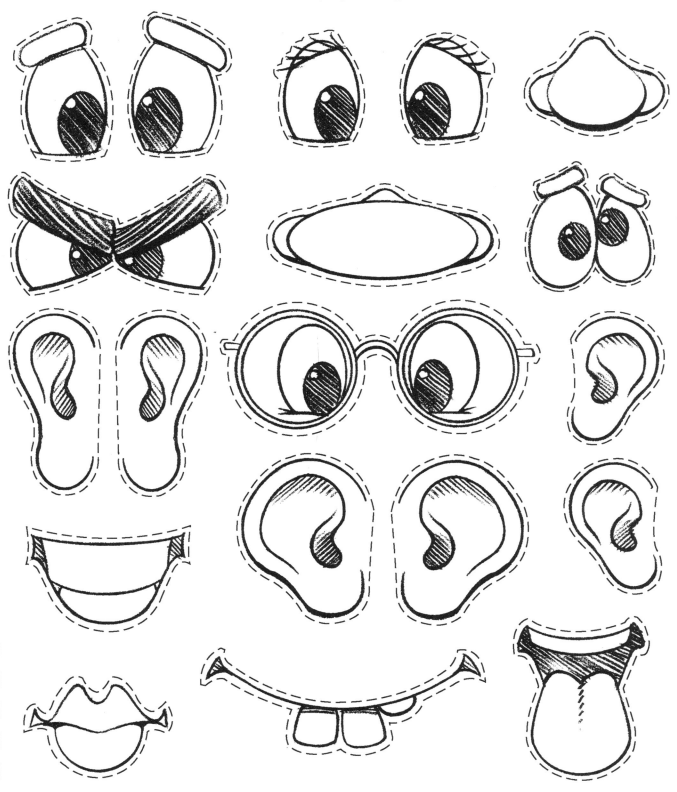

Patterning

Fill in the circle beside the picture that would come next.

Circles

Trace the **circles**.

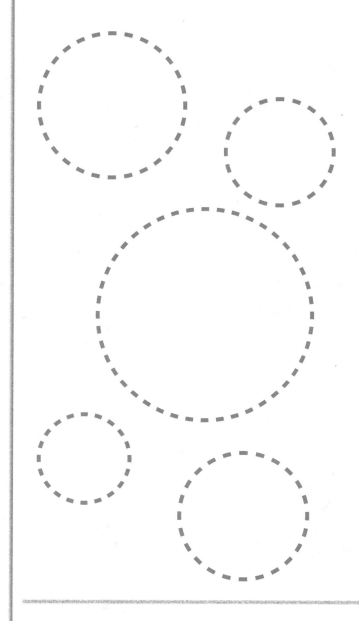

Can you find the **circles**?

How many?

Trace.

More Patterning

Draw shapes to continue the patterns. Color.

Squares

Trace the **squares**.

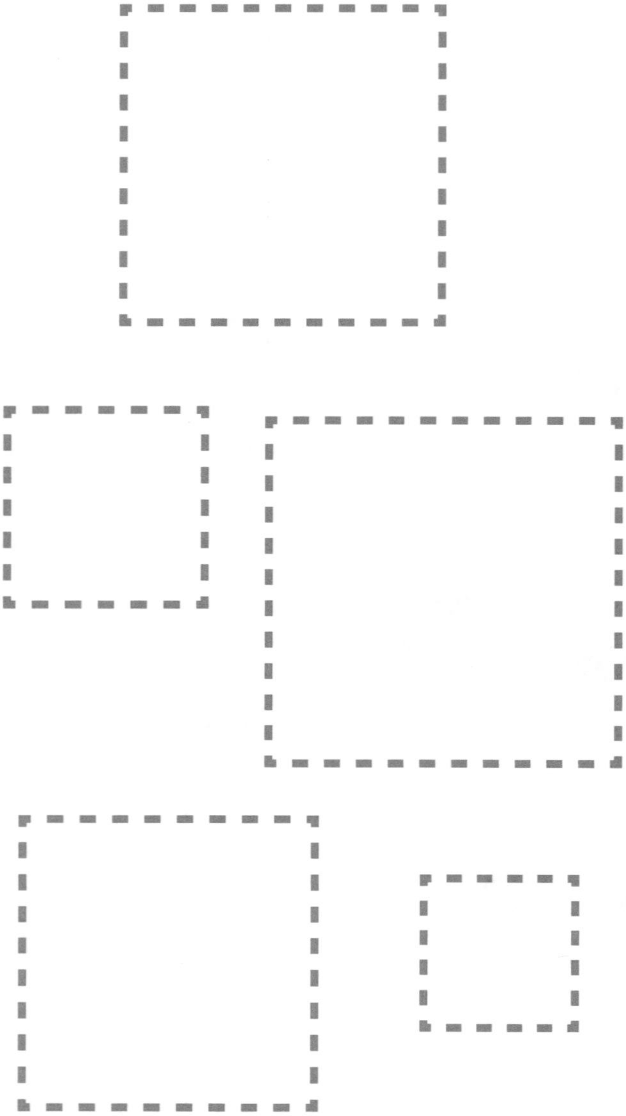

Can you find the **squares**?

How many?

Trace.

square square

Opposites

Draw a line between each pair of opposites.

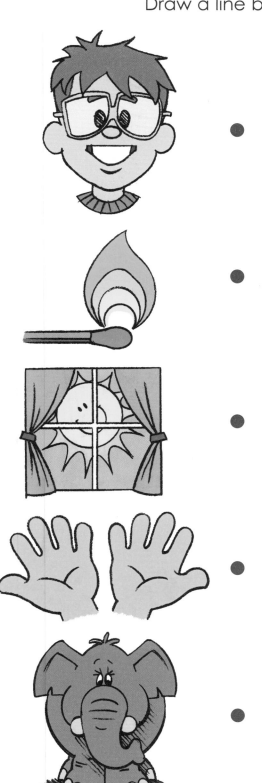

Triangles

Trace the **triangles**.

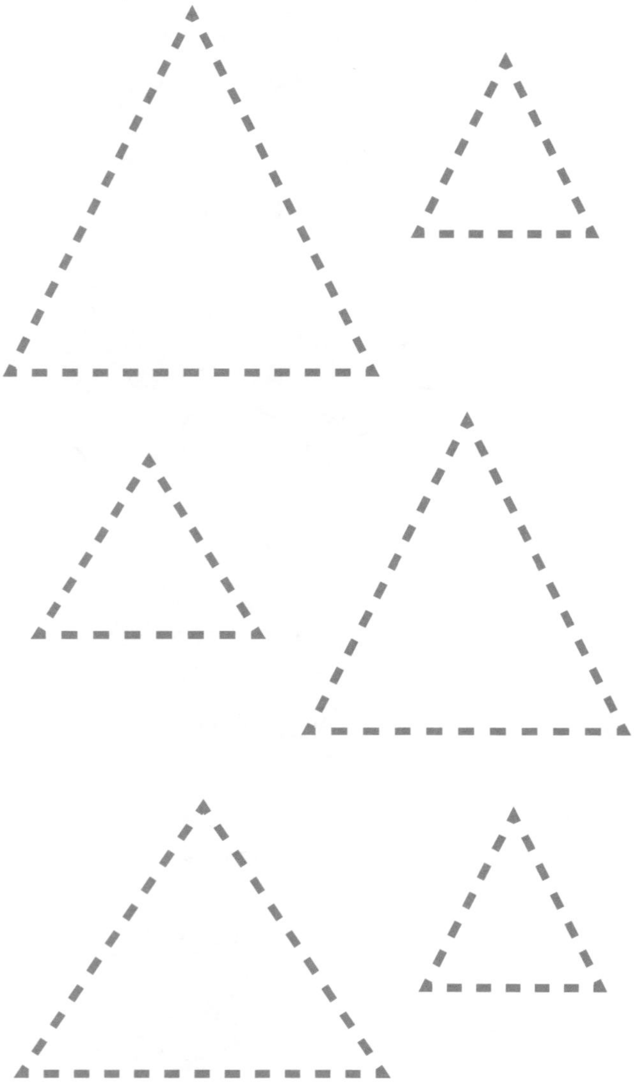

Can you find the **triangles**?

How many?

Trace.

triangle triangle

Concept of More

Count the sets in each box. Color the set that has **more**.

A.

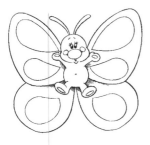

B.

C.

D.

Rectangles

Trace the **rectangles**.

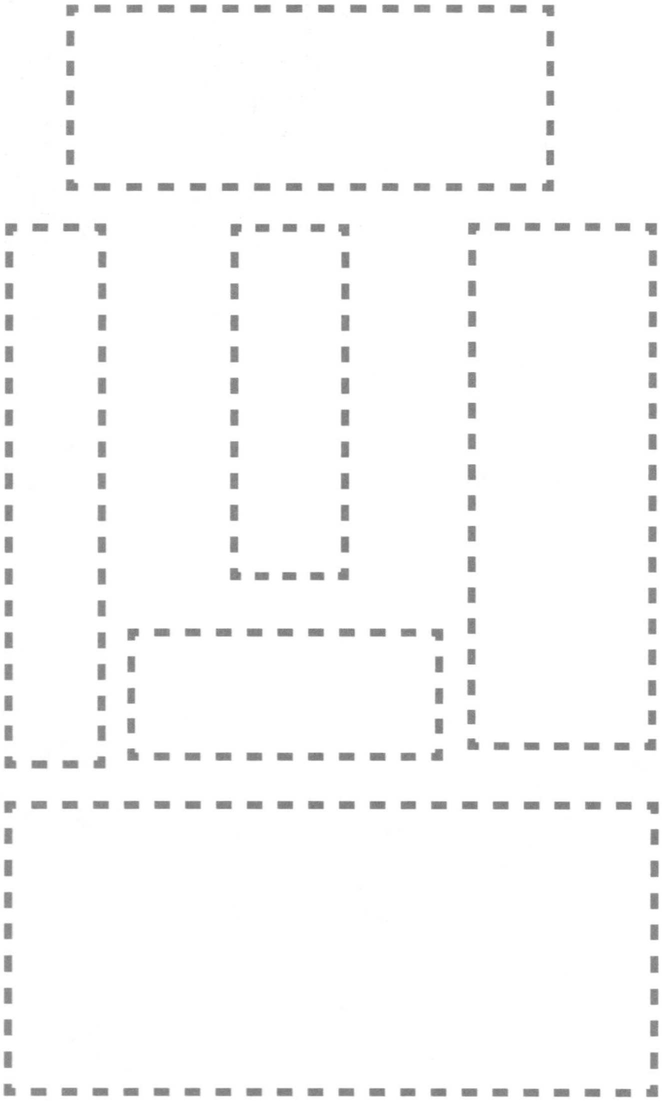

Can you find the **rectangles**?

How many?

Trace.

rectangle rectangle

Numbers 1–5

Count the animals. Circle the correct number.

   1   2   3   4   5

  1   2   3   4   5

    1   2   3   4   5

   1   2   3   4   5

 1   2   3   4   5

Hexagons

Trace the **hexagons**.

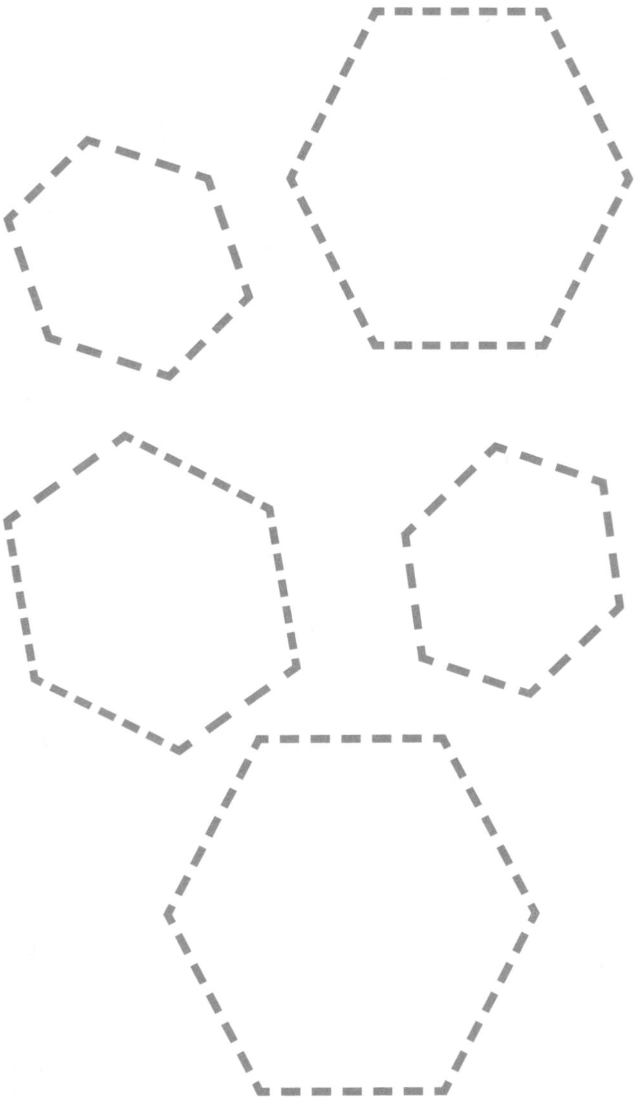

Can you find the **hexagons**?

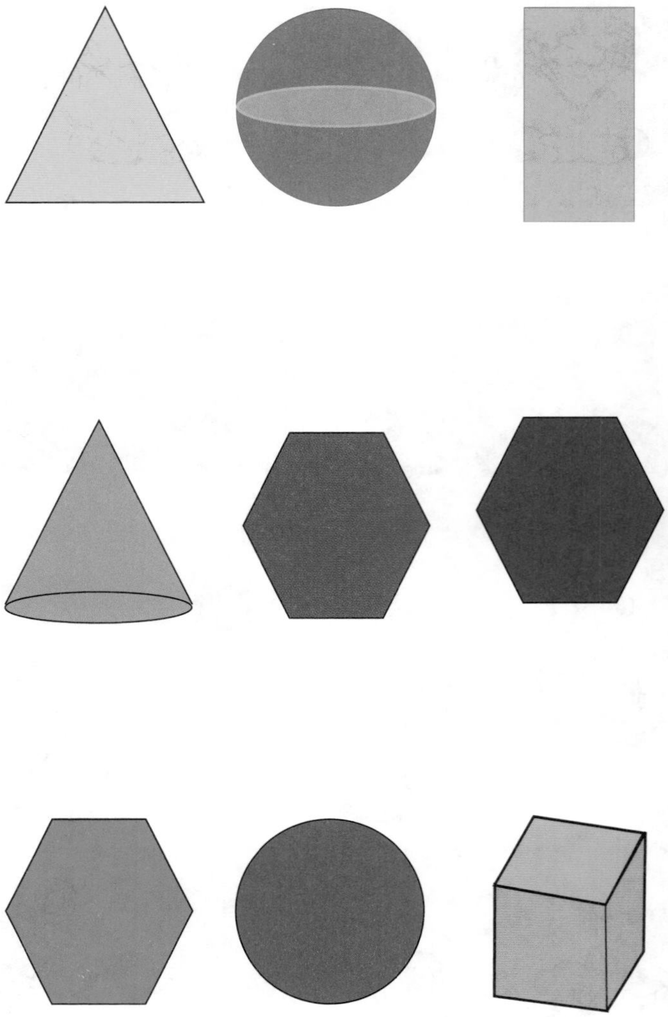

How many?

Trace.

hexagon hexagon

Numbers 1–10

Count the objects in each row. Print the number.

Cubes

Trace the **cubes**.

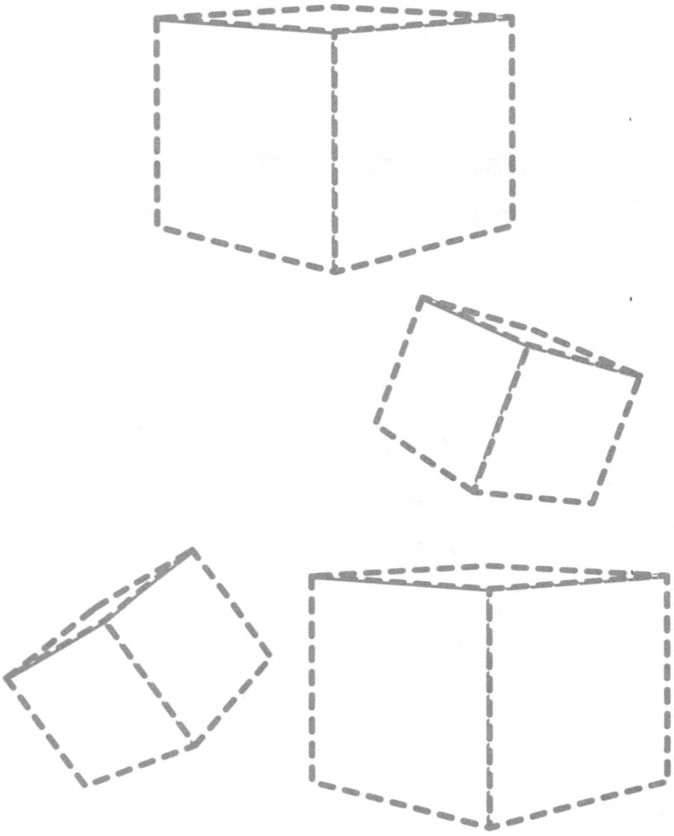

Find the **cube** in each row.

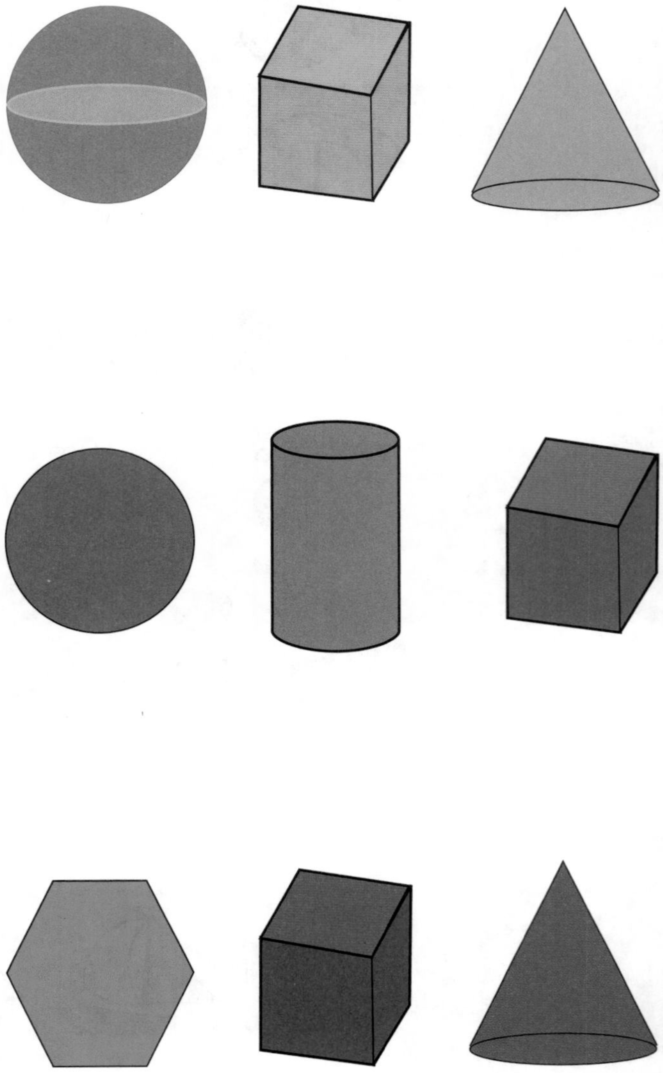

How many?

Trace.

cube cube cube

Graphing

We saw 6 monkeys, 4 lions, 3 polar bears, and 1 elephant at the zoo.
Color in the graph to show the animals we saw.

We saw the most _____.

Cylinders

Trace the **cylinders**.

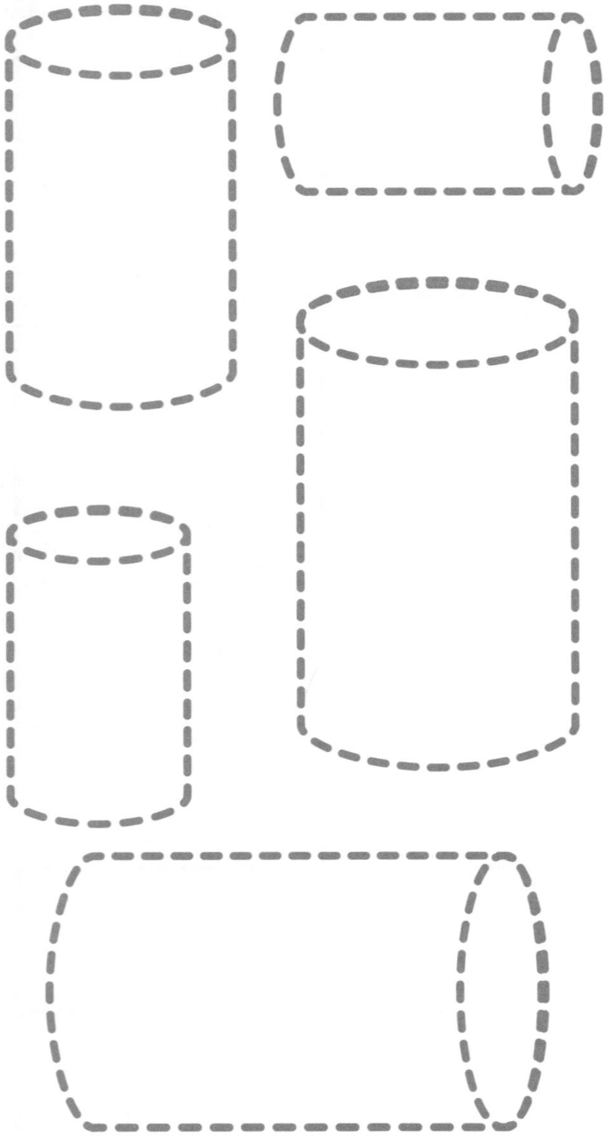

Can you find the **cylinders**?

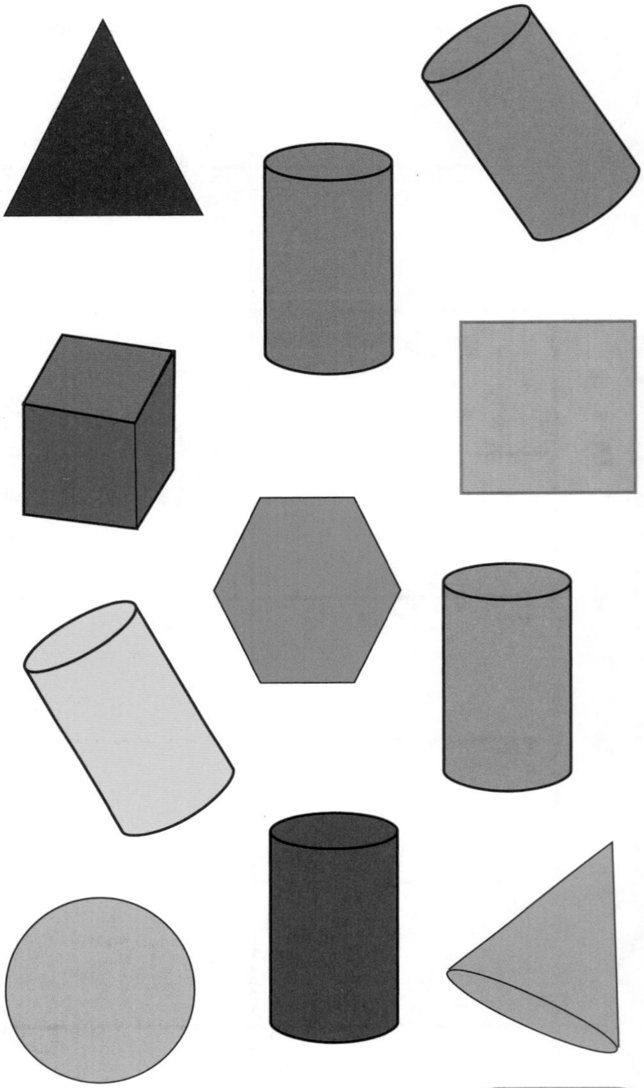

How many?

Trace.

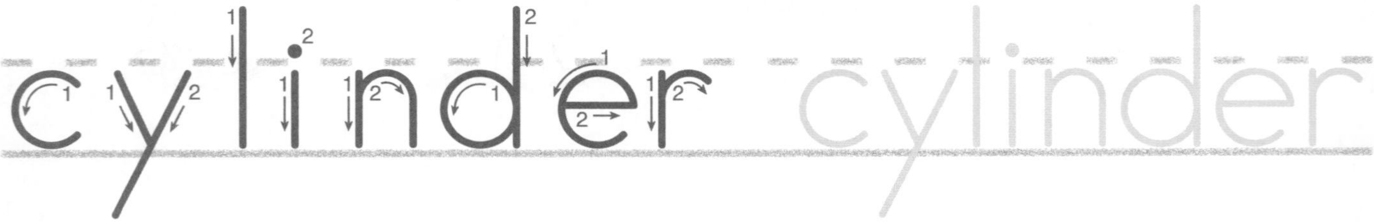

cylinder cylinder

Reading a Graph

Miss Larue's class made this graph showing their favorite fruits.
Study the graph and answer the questions.

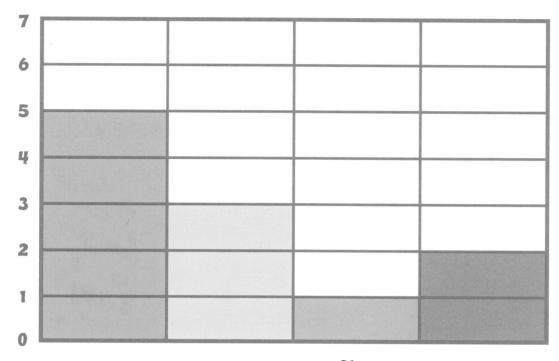

A. How many students like apples best?

B. How many students like bananas best?

C. How many students like strawberries best?

D. All together, how many students like bananas and grapes best?

29

Spheres

Trace the **spheres**.

Can you find the **spheres**?

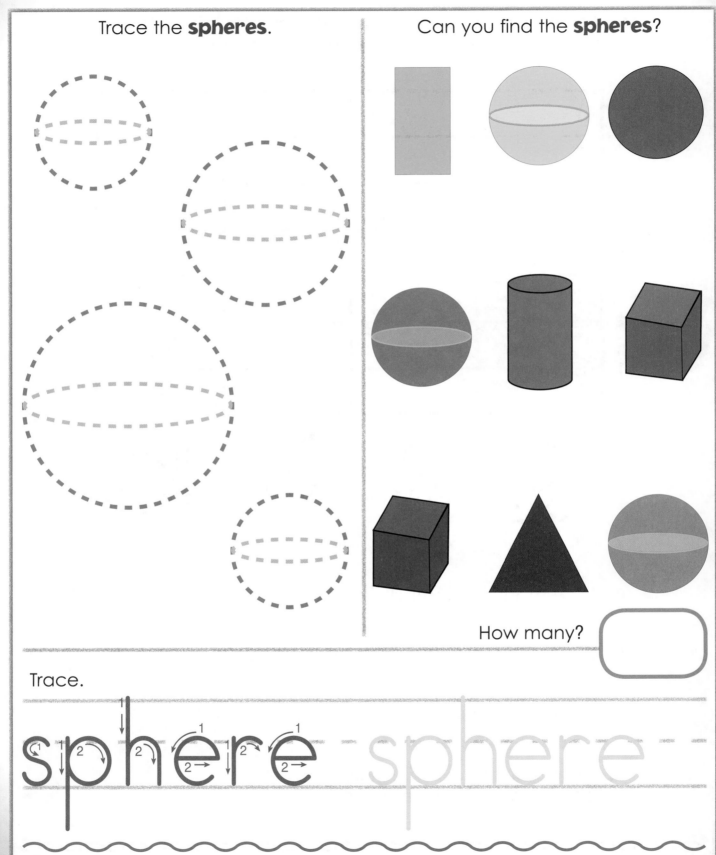

How many?

Trace.

sphere sphere

Game: Who Won the Race?

The **blue** car is 4th.   The **pink** car is 8th.
The **black** car is 7th.   The **purple** car is 10th.
The **green** car is 9th.   The **red** car is 2nd.
The **brown** car is 3rd.   The **yellow** car is 6th.
The **white** car is 5th.

Which car is 1st?   The _____ car

Color and cut out the cars. Glue onto the track following the clues.

red   blue   yellow   green   purple

orange   black   pink   white   brown

Remove pages 33-36. Cut along dashed lines. Staple pages in order.

ALL
ABOUT
ME!

This is a picture of me.

My name is:

1

Color the house.
Write your address on the lines at the bottom of the page.

3

Write your age on the card. Color.

2

Print your telephone number.

4

Draw a picture of
your favorite
television show
on the TV screen.

THIS ROOM
BELONGS TO

Print your first name on the line.
Color and cut out the sign.
Tape the sign to your bedroom door.

Draw a picture of your favorite animal.

The End

6

This section left blank for cutting activity on other side.

Shapes Assessment

Read the directions to your child.
Have your child color or point to the correct shape.

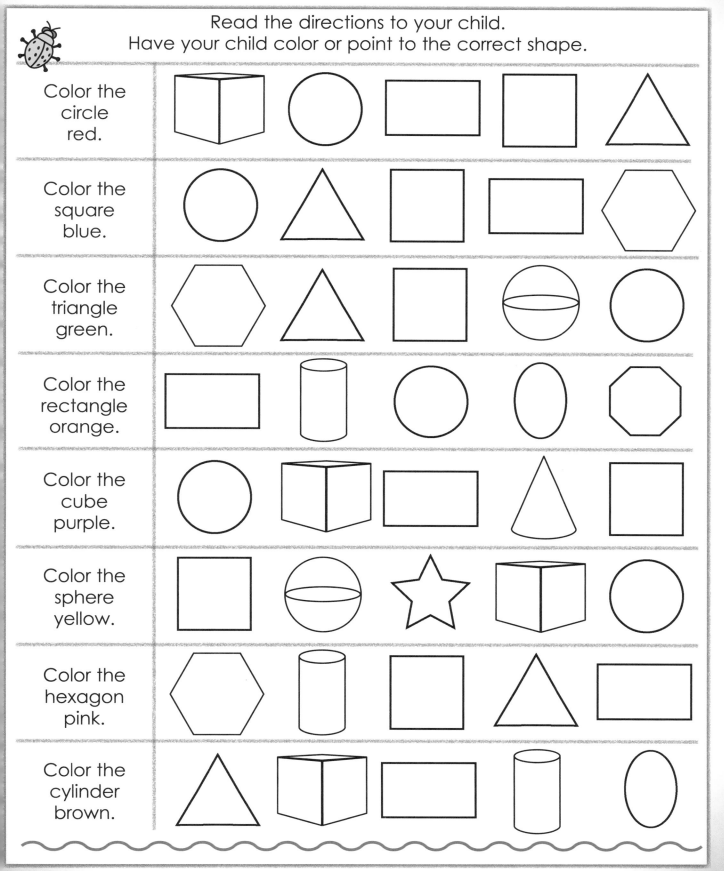

Color the circle red.

Color the square blue.

Color the triangle green.

Color the rectangle orange.

Color the cube purple.

Color the sphere yellow.

Color the hexagon pink.

Color the cylinder brown.

How Many?

Read the numeral at the beginning of each row.
Color that many shapes in the row.

3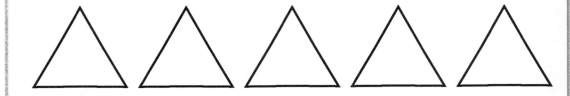

5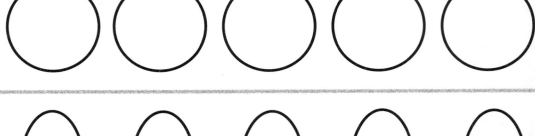

1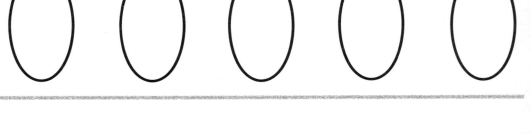

4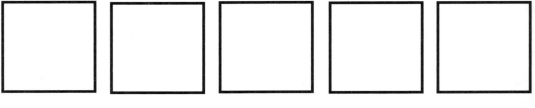

2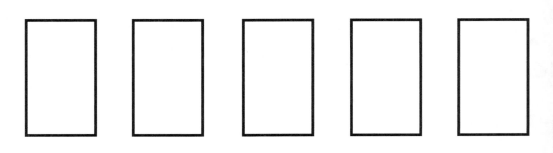

The Color Red

Color the things that are usually **red**.

Circle the words that spell **red**.

red	red	rem	red
red	reb	red	ned

Trace.

Count the Chocolate Chips

Count the chocolate chips. Write the number on the line.

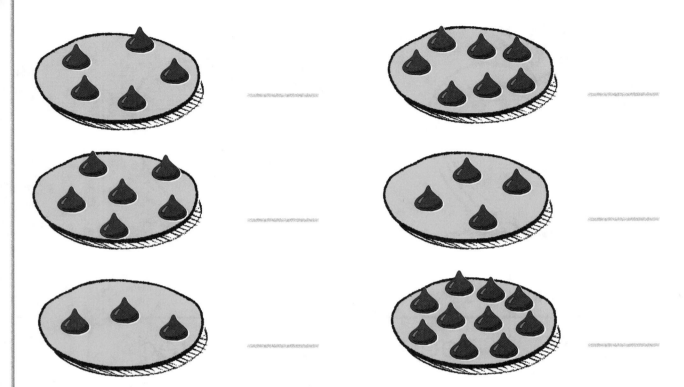

Draw the correct number of chocolate chips on each cookie.

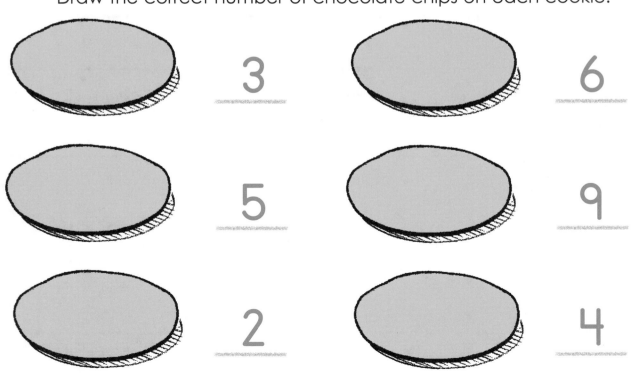

3

6

5

9

2

4

The Color Blue

Color the things that are usually **blue**.

Circle the words that spell **blue**.

blue	bhue	dlue	blue
bloe	blue	blue	blue

Trace.

Panda's Balloons

Count the dots. Color the balloons:

6 = blue   **7 = green**   **8 = orange**   **9 = purple**   **10 = yellow**

Color the panda, too!

The Color Yellow

Color the things that are usually yellow.

Circle the words that spell yellow.

yellow	yellow	mellow	yellow
yallow	yellow	yellow	yullaw

Trace.

yellow   yellow

Try your own.

Dot-to-Dot 1–10

Connect the dots to make a picture.
Begin at the numeral **1**. Continue in **numerical order**.

The Color Green

Color the things that are usually **green**.

Circle the words that spell **green**.

green	jrean	green	preem
grean	green	green	green

Trace.

Try your own.

Order of Numbers 1–10

Put a counter (such as a penny) on each ant. Count aloud starting with 1.

Write the numbers 1–10.
Each number is 1 more than the one before.

Write the number that comes next.   Write the number that comes first.

1, 2, _____   _____ , 7, 8

3, 4, _____   _____ , 9, 10

5, 6, _____   _____ , 2, 3

Write the missing numbers.

0, 1, ___, 3, ___, 5, 6, ___, ___, 9, ___

The Color Orange

Color the things that are usually **orange**.

Circle the words that spell **orange**.

orange   orange   orange   oranje

orauge   orange   oranpe   orange

Trace.

Measuring in Inches

Look at each ruler. Write the length of each object.

A. _____ inches

B. _____ inch

C. _____ inches

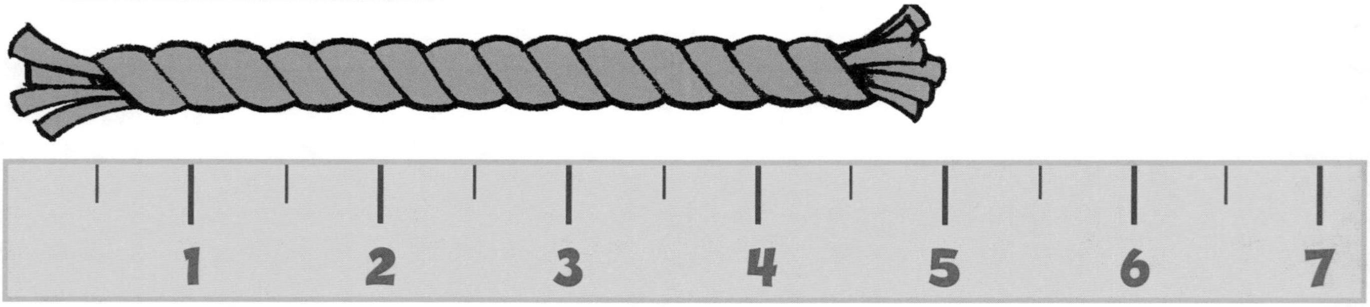

D. _____ inches

The Color Purple

Color the things that are usually **purple**.

Circle the words that spell **purple**.

purple	purple	purple	parple
purdle	purpel	purple	purple

Trace.

Try your own.

Tallest, Shortest, Longest

Color the **shortest** one red.
Color the **longest** one yellow.

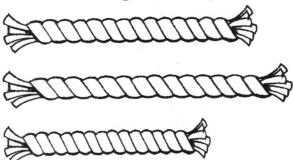

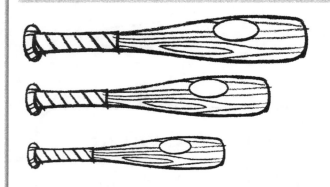

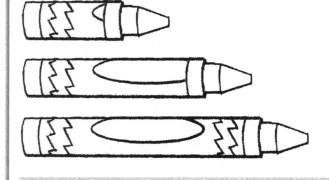

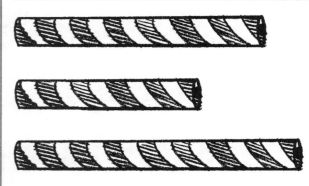

Draw an **X** on the tallest one.
Circle the shortest one.

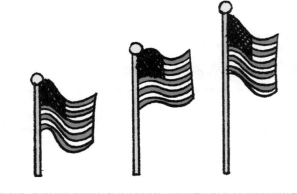

The Color Brown

Color the things that are usually **brown**.

 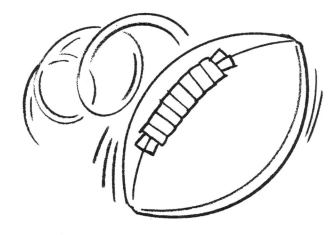

Circle the words that spell **brown**.

brown	brown	drown	brown
broan	brown	brown	prown

Trace.

Try your own.

What's Missing?

Color the pictures. Find 8 things in the top picture that are missing from the bottom picture. Circle them.

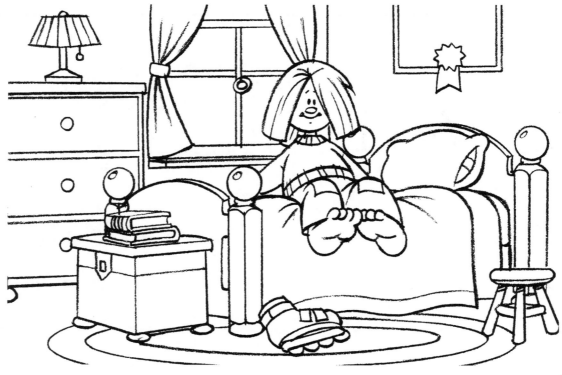

The Color Black

Color the things that are usually **black**.

Circle the words that spell **black**.

black	blach	black	plack
dlach	black	black	black

Trace.

Try your own.

Equal Size

Look at the first picture in each row.
Circle the picture in the row that is the **same size** as the first picture.

The Color White

Color the things that are usually white.

Circle the words that spell white.

wtihe	white	white	wyite
white	withe	white	white

Trace.

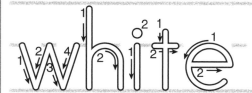 

Dot-to-Dot 1–25

Connect the dots from **1** to **25** to make an animal.

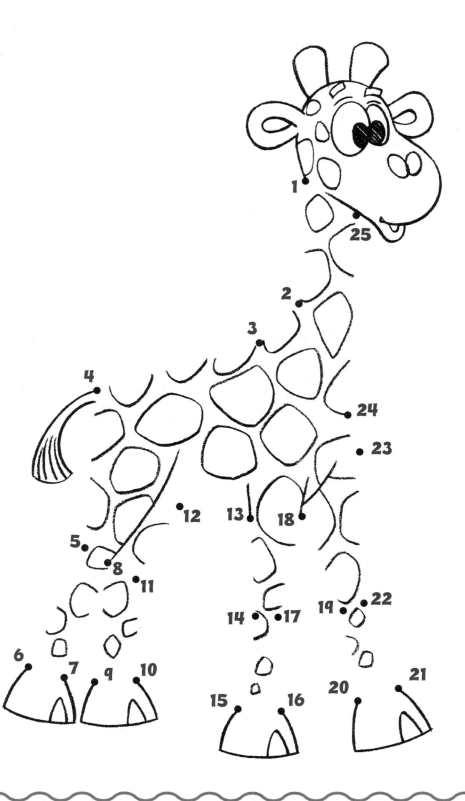

The Color Pink

Color the things that are usually **pink**.

Circle the words that spell **pink**.

pink	pink	bink	tink
pink	qink	pink	pink

Trace.

pink pink

Try your own.

Following Directions

Parent: Read the directions to your child.

1. Color the clown's hair **orange**.
2. Color his hat **purple**.
3. Color his shoes **red**.

4. Color his dog **brown** with **black** spots.
5. Color the squares on his clothes **green**, the circles **blue**, and the triangles **yellow**.

Game: Color Memory Match

Color the pictures and cut out the cards. Match each color word to the correct picture.

green	black			
yellow	white			
blue	purple	pink		
red	orange	brown		

3

Color by number.

1 = black   4 = red

2 = green   5 = brown

3 = yellow

1

GAMES AND PUZZLES

A "Finish-It-Yourself" Book

Name: _____

Find and circle the words.
The words can be found across and down.

Word List

one   two   three   four

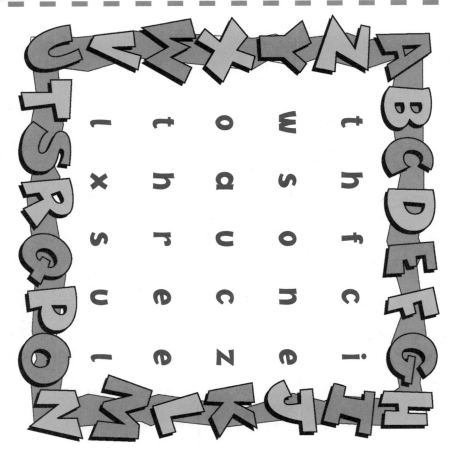

t	h	f	c	i
w	s	o	n	e
o	a	u	c	z
t	h	r	e	e
l	x	s	u	l

4

Help Billy Bear find t he honey.

2

7

Trace the dashed lines to complete the clown. Color the picture.

Color by number.

I = yellow

2 = black

3 = red

4 = purple

8

Connect the dots from **A** to **H**.
Color the picture.

A
B
F
E
G
C
D
H

9

Find and circle **10** things to eat.

64

My Parents and Me: Painting Fun

Here are some painting ideas that you and your child will enjoy.
Keep in mind that painting outside makes for easy cleanup!

Marble Painting

You will need: white construction paper, a cookie sheet or 9" x 12" cake pan, liquid tempera paint, and marbles.
Directions: Place a piece of construction paper on the cookie sheet or in the bottom of the cake pan. Let your child squeeze a few drops of liquid tempera paint onto the paper. Set one or two marbles on the paper. Have your child hold the pan and gently roll the marbles back and forth to create beautiful designs.

Sensory Finger Painting

This easy finger paint recipe is unique because it provides additional sensory experience for a young child. The paint has a grainy quality that is unlike other finger paints. It is a wonderful paint to use to practice handwriting.
You will need: 1 cup flour, 1½ teaspoons salt or sand, 1 cup water, and liquid tempera paint.
Directions: Add several drops of tempera paint to the water. Combine the flour and salt or sand in a mixing bowl, then add the water slowly. Stir until blended. Make several different colors of paint, if desired.

Window Painting

During the month of December, it is common to see various designs and greetings of the season painted on windows. Here is an easy recipe you can use to paint windows any time of the year. Paint hearts for Valentine's Day, bunnies and eggs for Easter, or pumpkins and bats for Halloween.
You will need: equal parts Bon Ami cleanser, Alabastrine (glass paint that comes in a powder and can be purchased at most paint or hardware stores), and dry tempera paint.
Directions: Mix the ingredients together. Add enough water to make a creamy paste. Paint on the window with a small brush or rag. The window paint will wipe off easily with a damp cloth and will not stain the glass.

Fabric Painting

You can create many interesting projects on fabric: decorate white T-shirts as gifts or just for fun, design ties for grandpa or dad, make fabric wall hangings—the possibilities are endless! Here is one successful fabric paint recipe to try with your child.
You will need: 1 cup powdered albumen (or egg white), 3 cups liquid tempera paint, a few drops of vinegar, and a stiff brush.
Directions: Add the powdered albumen to the liquid tempera paint and mix together. Add a few drops of vinegar. Use a stiff brush to apply the paint to the fabric.

IMPORTANT NOTE: *To set the colors, place the fabric facedown between two pieces of paper and steam with a hot iron. The paint will set, but it is still suggested that you wash the fabric separately or with a dark load the first time you wash it.*

The Letter Aa

apple

Trace and print.

Trace and print.

Circle the pictures that have the **short** Aa sound. Draw an X on the pictures with the **long** Aa sound.

Introduction to Addition

Count the objects in each row. Write the total.
Read each problem as a number sentence.

(1   plus   1   equals)

The Letter Bb

Bb

ball

Trace and print.

B B B

Trace and print.

b b b

Color the pictures that start with the **Bb** sound.

Circle each **B** and **b**.

B   b   B

E   B   d

D

b   b

Using Counters to Add

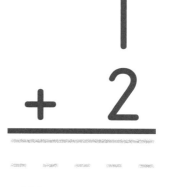

Place counters (such as pennies) next to each numeral.
Count and add. Write your answer on the line.

$$\begin{array}{r} 1 \\ + 1 \\ \hline \end{array}$$

$$\begin{array}{r} 2 \\ + 1 \\ \hline \end{array}$$

$$\begin{array}{r} 1 \\ + 2 \\ \hline \end{array}$$

$$\begin{array}{r} 1 \\ + 3 \\ \hline \end{array}$$

$$\begin{array}{r} 3 \\ + 2 \\ \hline \end{array}$$

$$\begin{array}{r} 5 \\ + 0 \\ \hline \end{array}$$

$$\begin{array}{r} 4 \\ + 1 \\ \hline \end{array}$$

$$\begin{array}{r} 0 \\ + 4 \\ \hline \end{array}$$

$$\begin{array}{r} 3 \\ + 1 \\ \hline \end{array}$$

The Letter Cc

cat

Trace and print.

C C C C

Trace and print.

C C C

Color the pictures that start with the Cc sound.

Circle each C and c.

C   c   e

D   C   c

    c   O   c

How Many More?

How many more mice are needed?
Write the correct number of mice in each box.

+ [ ] = **8**

+ [ ] = **10**

+ [ ] = **5**

+ [ ] = **q**

+ [ ] = **6**

+ [ ] = **7**

The Letter Dd

D d

duck

Trace and print.

D D D D

Trace and print.

d d d

Color the pictures that start with the **Dd** sound.

Circle each **D** and **d**.

P   D   d

d   D   d

D   b

p

Chilly Sums to 10

Model the addition problems. Use the penguins and counters.
Write the sums.

2 + 2 = ___   1 + 4 = ___   0 + 3 = ___   1 + 5 = ___

1	6	4	3	5	3
+ 1	+ 2	+ 0	+ 6	+ 5	+ 2

7 + 0 = ___   3 + 4 = ___   4 + 5 = ___   0 + 0 = ___

The Letter Ee

E e

elephant

Trace and print.

Trace and print.

Circle the pictures that have the **short Ee** sound. Draw an X on the pictures with the **long Ee** sound.

Numbers 11–20

How many?

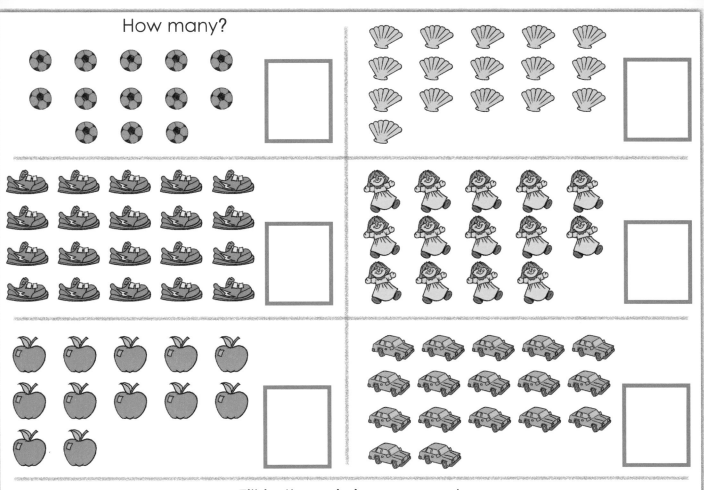

Fill in the missing numeral.

10, ☐, 12   15, ☐, 17   16, ☐, 18

16, 17, ☐   ☐, 15, 16   18, 19, ☐

11, 12, ☐   11, ☐, 13   14, ☐, 16

Capitalization

Circle the capital letter that starts each sentence.

Jen and Matt go to the zoo.

They see lots of animals.

Jen likes the tigers.

Matt likes the zebras.

Write the word in the box on the line. Use a capital letter.

| dogs | _____ can bark. |

| i | _____ like ice cream. |

| ben | _____ plays soccer. |

| the | _____ moon is bright. |

Game: Animal Addition

Color and cut out the animal squares. Use them to make number sentences of facts to 5. Lay out a sentence and practice reading it out loud.

Here are the facts to 5 as a guide.

1 + 1 = 2   2 + 2 = 4   3 + 1 = 4   4 + 1 = 5
1 + 2 = 3   2 + 3 = 5   3 + 2 = 5
1 + 3 = 4   2 + 1 = 3
1 + 4 = 5

Example:

2   +   1   =   3

RHYME TIME

A "Finish-It-Yourself" Book

Parent reads aloud to the child.
Child and parent decide which words rhyme.
Child copies words from the word list on the lines.

1

This is my _____ .

She is very _____ .

She'll never run _____ .

She just sleeps all _____ .

Word List

fat   away
cat   day

3

Howard is a _____ .

He lives in a _____ .

He flies with _____ .

Be careful! He _____ .

Word List

wings	bee
tree	stings

2

Look at the _____ .

He's dancing a _____ .

With bells on his _____ ,

he won't miss a _____ .

Word List

jig	beat
feet	pig

4

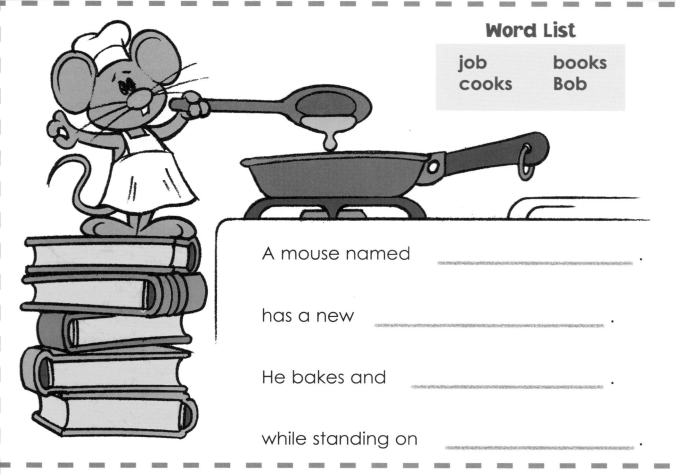

Word List

Word List

job	books
cooks	Bob

A mouse named _____.

has a new _____.

He bakes and _____.

while standing on _____.

5

Hello, I'm a _____.

I live in a _____.

My friends came to _____.

my giant _____.

Word List

jug	see
TV	bug

7

Up, up, and away in my _____,

I'm flying all the way to the _____.

Look at the stars,
    the planets, and the _____.

What a day! I had so much _____.

Word List

moon	sun
fun	balloon

6

Word List

friend	cry
bye	end

I must say good-_____.

Please don't _____.

Because this, my _____,

is the _____.

8

Measuring with a Ruler

Cut along the dashed lines.
Use the ruler to measure the length of each object.

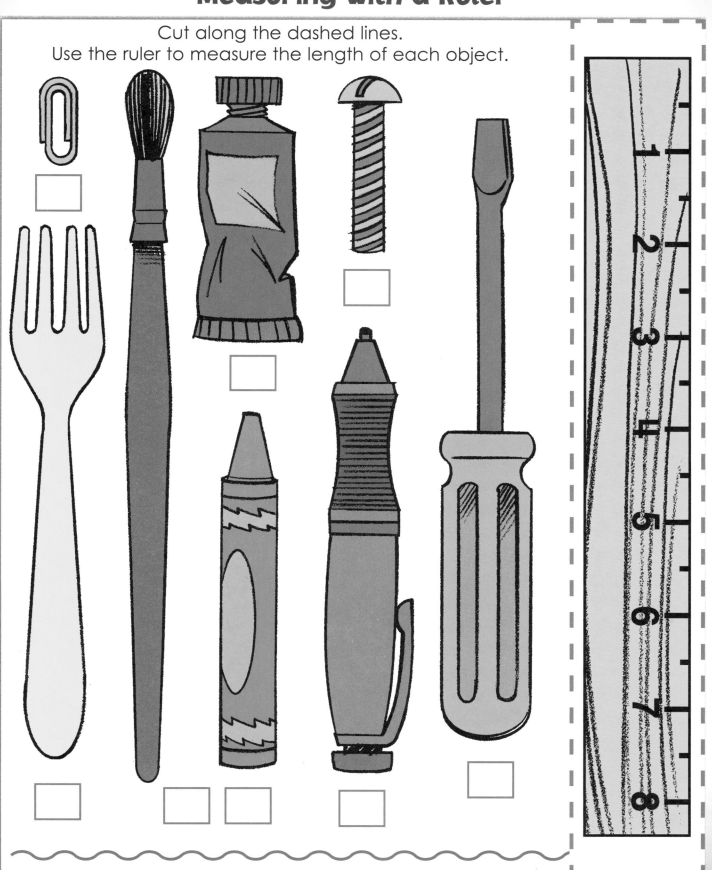

The Letter Ff

fish

Trace and print.

Trace and print.

Color the pictures that start with the Ff sound.

Circle each F and f.

F   f   E

F   F

f

f   G   g

Identifying Coins and Values

Look at the coin in each box. Circle the correct amount.

1¢   5¢   10¢   25¢

1¢   5¢   10¢   25¢

1¢   5¢   10¢   25¢

1¢   5¢   10¢   25¢

The Letter Gg

goat

Trace and print.

G   G   G

Trace and print.

g   g   g

Color the pictures that start with the **Gg** sound.

Circle each **G** and **g**.

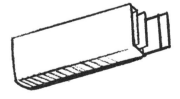

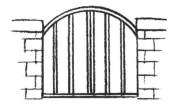  

p   G   g

g   G   O

G

C   g

Pennies for Piggy

Count the pennies. Write the amount on each piggy bank.

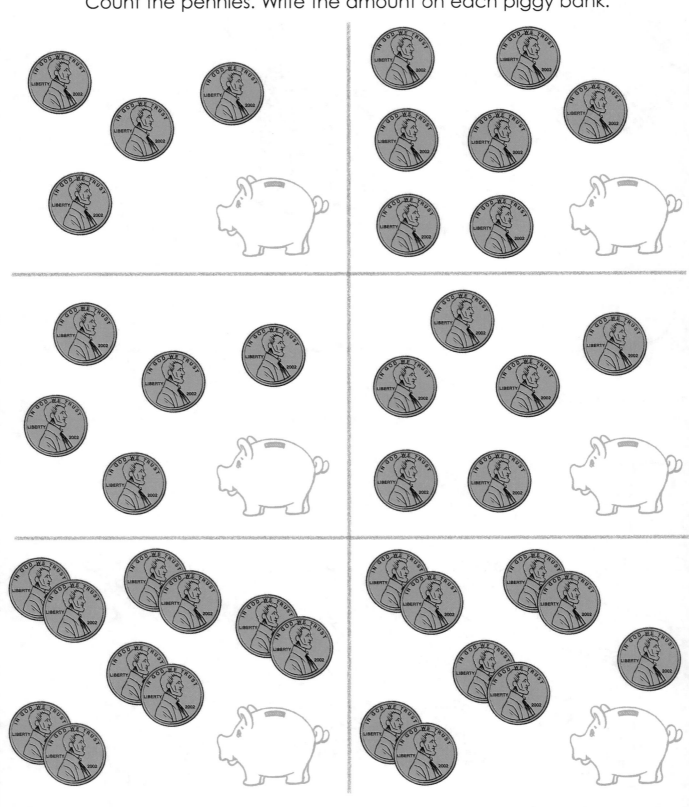

The Letter Hh

horse

Trace and print.

Trace and print.

Color the pictures that start with the **Hh** sound.

Circle each **H** and **h**.

d   H   h

b   H

h   E

H

      h

Adding Nickels and Pennies

Add the pennies to the nickel in the piggy bank.
Write the total. Color the banks.

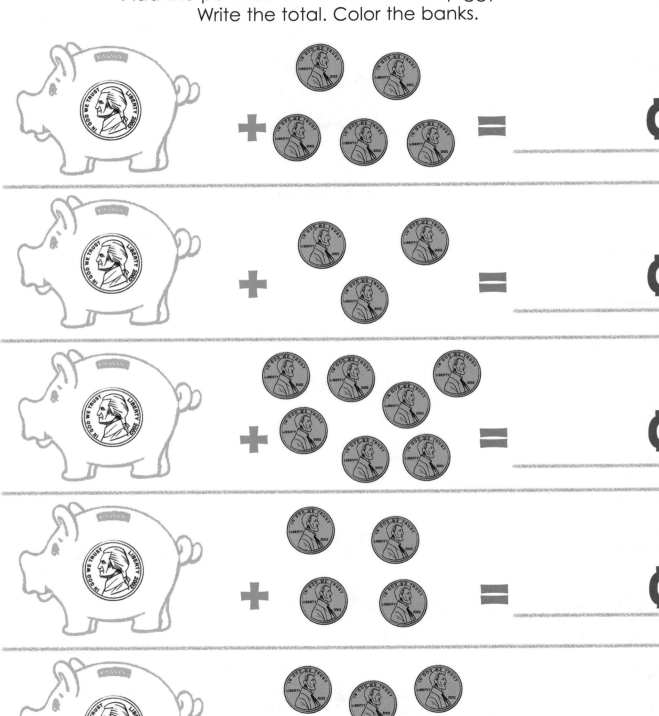

The Letter Ii

igloo

Trace and print.

Trace and print.

Circle the pictures that have the **short Ii** sound. Draw an **X** on the pictures with the **long Ii** sound.

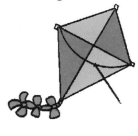

Domino Addition

Add the dots on each domino. Write out the number sentence.

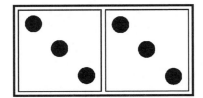

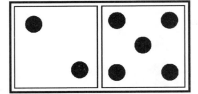

$+$ _____ $=$ _____

$+$ _____ $=$ _____

$+$ _____ $=$ _____

$+$ _____ $=$ _____

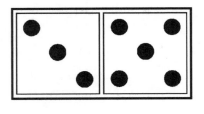

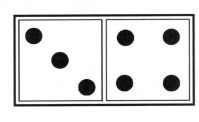

$+$ _____ $=$ _____

$+$ _____ $=$ _____

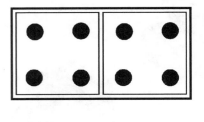

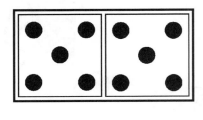

$+$ _____ $=$ _____

$+$ _____ $=$ _____

Identifying and Counting Money

Match the coins to their **names**.

 nickel

 quarter

 penny

dime

Match the coins to their **amounts**.

 10¢

 25¢

 1¢

 5¢

How much money is in each piggy bank?

A. _____ ¢   B. _____ ¢

The Letter Jj

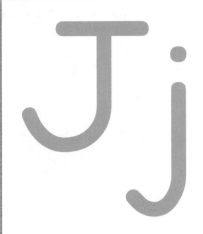

jar

Trace and print.

J

Trace and print.

j

Color the pictures that start with the Jj sound.

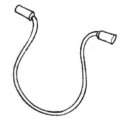

Circle each J and j.

J   q   j

O   J

j   p

J   j

Number Review 0–20

Write the number that comes next.

3, 4, 5, _____   2, 3, 4, _____

12, 13, 14, _____   16, 17, 18, _____

9, 10, 11, _____   7, 8, 9, _____

1, 2, 3, _____   0, 1, 2, _____

Write the numbers from **1** to **20**.

Punctuation

Circle the period in each sentence.

Seth has a garden.

He grows carrots.

Sam picks flowers.

The flowers are purple.

Write a question mark at the end of each question.

Do you like carrots _____

What is for dinner _____

Can I have a flower _____

Where is the watering can _____

My "Great Job" Chart

Color one square each time you do one of the jobs below.

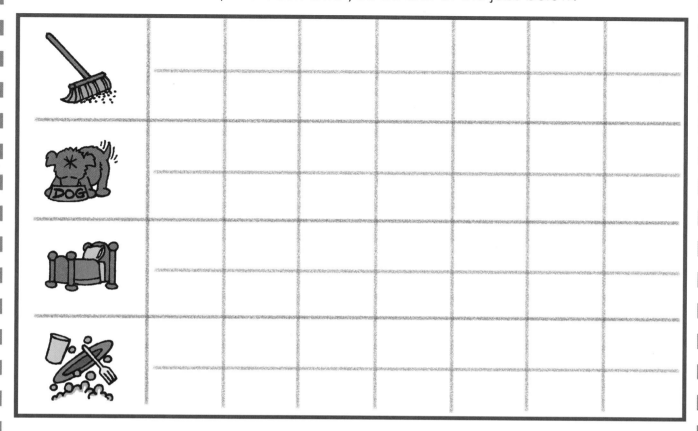

Color and cut out the crown below. Glue a strip of paper to each side of the crown base. Fit the crown to your head. Staple the strips of paper together.

I AM "BEARY" SPECIAL

KINDERGARTEN WAS FUN!

A book about _____'s

(your name)

year in kindergarten

This was my kindergarten teacher.

This was my best friend in kindergarten.

Name: _____

Name: _____

This is me. My name is _____

Look at all the fun things I did in kindergarten.

2

This was our playground.
My favorite playground activity was _____

Color the playground.

4

**We listened to many stories in kindergarten.
My favorite story was:**

Draw the cover.

I learned to read some words.
Write the words.

5

I learned my colors.
Color.

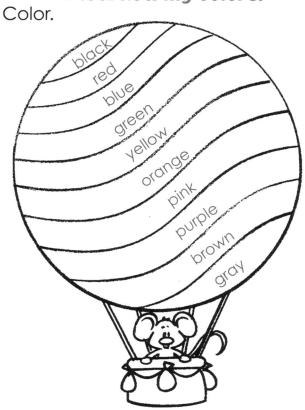

black
red
blue
green
yellow
orange
pink
purple
brown
gray

I know my shapes.
Trace.

square

rectangle

star

circle

diamond

octagon

triangle

7

101

I learned my numbers.

Connect the dots.

I am a number

_____ !

I know my alphabet letters.

A	e	N	r
B	g	O	v
C	g	P	n
D	b	Q	w
E	i	R	s
F	a	S	x
G	h	T	o
H	c	U	u
I	k	V	p
J	f	W	t
K	l	X	q
L	d	Y	z
M	m	Z	y
	j		

6

The best thing about kindergarten was:

Congratulations, Kindergarten Graduate!

You are officially going into 1st grade!

The End

8

Help the Seal Solve the Problems

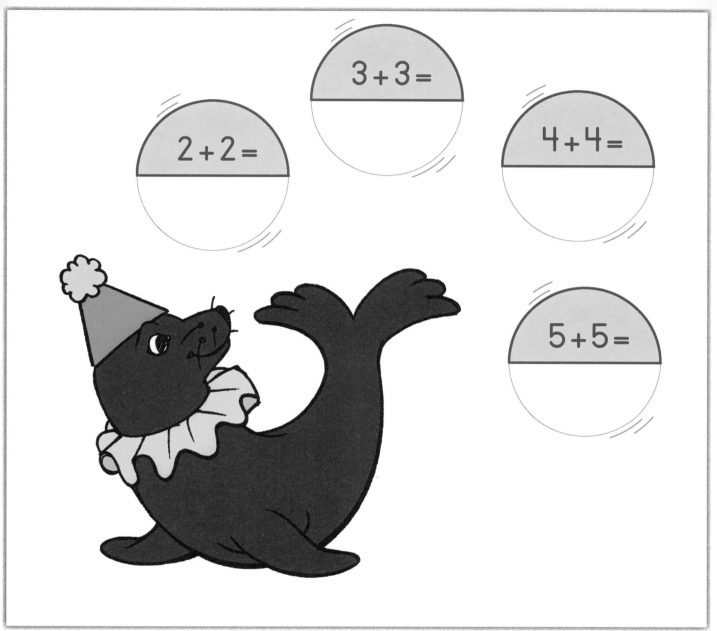

$3 + 3 =$

$2 + 2 =$

$4 + 4 =$

$5 + 5 =$

Cut and paste the correct answer under each problem.

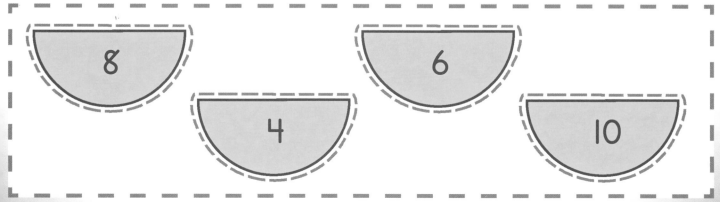

8

6

4

10

The Letter Kk

king

Trace and print.

Trace and print.

Color the pictures that start with the **Kk** sound.

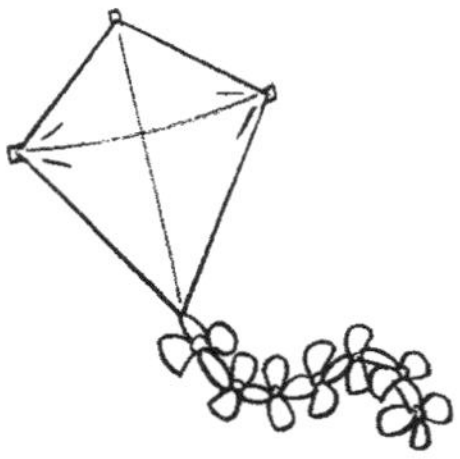

Circle each **K** and **k**.

K   K   h

K   k   V

k   L   k

A Gigantic Puzzle

Solve each problem.

$4 + 1 = $ _5_ $4 + 3 = $ ____

$2 + 2 = $ ____ $3 + 3 = $ ____

$3 + 1 = $ ____ $0 + 3 = $ ____

$1 + 1 = $ ____ $2 + 5 = $ ____

$4 + 4 = $ ____ $1 + 7 = $ ____

Now use + and = to mark the same problems hidden on the elephant.

Hint

Problems can also go like this:

$$\begin{array}{r} 0 \\ + 0 \\ \hline 0 \end{array}$$

The Letter Ll

lion

Trace and print.

Trace and print.

Color the pictures that start with the Ll sound.

Circle each L and l.

I   I

L   i

I   l

I   L

Addition to 10

Show each butterfly to its branch.

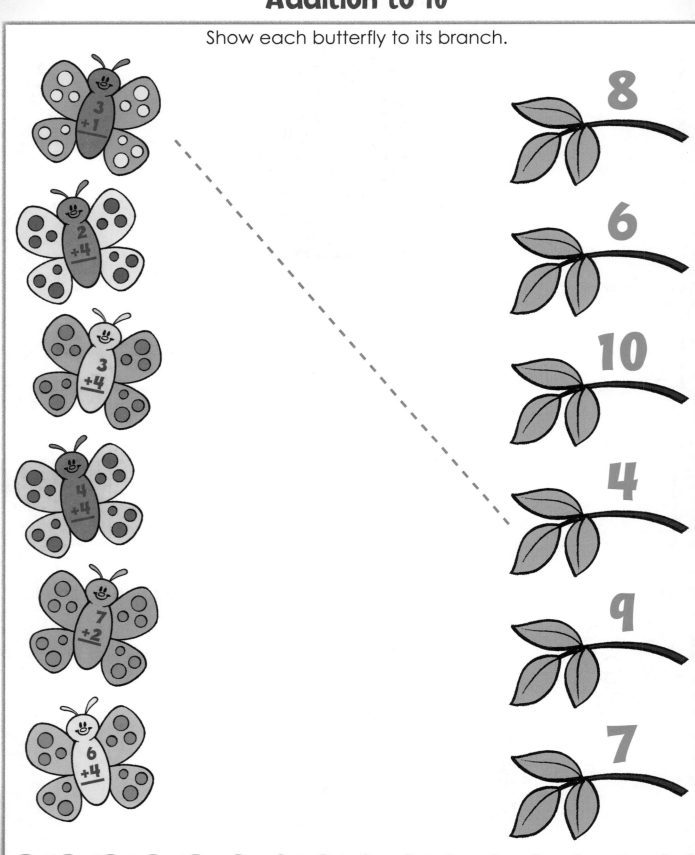

The Letter Mm

mouse

Trace and print.

Trace and print.

Color the pictures that start with the **M**m sound.

Circle each **M** and **m**.

M   N   M

n   M   m

m   m   n

Apple Addition

Solve the problems.

$$4 + 5$$

$$0 + 1$$

$$3 + 6$$

$$1 + 8$$

$$0 + 9$$

$$6 + 3$$

$$1 + 5$$

$$7 + 2$$

$$2 + 4$$

The Letter Nn

newt

Trace and print.

Trace and print.

Color the pictures that start with the N n sound.

Circle each N and n.

N   n   m

N   n   M

n   m   N

Addition Assessment

Find each sum. Use counters (such as pennies) as needed.

$$\begin{array}{r} 1 \\ + 1 \\ \hline \end{array}$$
$$\begin{array}{r} 2 \\ + 3 \\ \hline \end{array}$$
$$\begin{array}{r} 2 \\ + 2 \\ \hline \end{array}$$
$$\begin{array}{r} 1 \\ + 4 \\ \hline \end{array}$$

$$\begin{array}{r} 3 \\ + 1 \\ \hline \end{array}$$
$$\begin{array}{r} 5 \\ + 2 \\ \hline \end{array}$$
$$\begin{array}{r} 4 \\ + 3 \\ \hline \end{array}$$
$$\begin{array}{r} 5 \\ + 5 \\ \hline \end{array}$$

$$\begin{array}{r} 6 \\ + 0 \\ \hline \end{array}$$
$$\begin{array}{r} 2 \\ + 1 \\ \hline \end{array}$$
$$\begin{array}{r} 3 \\ + 6 \\ \hline \end{array}$$
$$\begin{array}{r} 5 \\ + 3 \\ \hline \end{array}$$

Action Words

Circle the words that are action words.

swim

run

umbrella

jar

fish

eat

cook

sew

Addition Quiz

How many addition problems can you solve correctly?

A.

6	3	1	6
+ 1	+ 4	+ 5	+ 0

B.

7	3	2	5
+ 1	+ 2	+ 2	+ 5

C.

3	4	4	3
+ 6	+ 2	+ 6	+ 3

D.

3	10
+ 5	+ 0

9	7
+ 1	+ 2

correct / 16 total

Number Words One to Five

Trace. Color.
Draw a line to match the number to the correct picture.

1 one

2 two

3 three

4 four

5 five

The Letter Oo

octopus

Trace and print.

Trace and print.

Circle the pictures that have the **short Oo** sound. Draw an **X** on the pictures with the **long Oo** sound.

Number Words Six to Ten

Trace. Color. Draw a line to match the number to the correct picture.

6 six

7 seven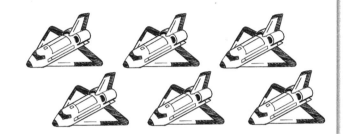

8 eight

9 nine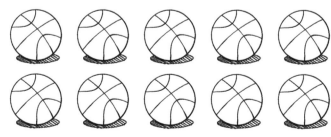

10 ten

The Letter Pp

penguin

Trace and print.

P   P   P

Trace and print.

p   p   p

Color the pictures that start with the **Pp** sound.

Circle each **P** and **p**.

P   P   p

p   q   P

b   p   D

p

Color by Number Words

Color the clown using the code.

1 = blue	2 = yellow	3 = red	4 = orange	5 = green

Letter Review A–P

Write the missing letters.

A a _____   b _____   c _____   D

_____   e   F   G   h _____

i _____   J   k _____   L

m _____   N   O   p _____

Circle the correct beginning sound.

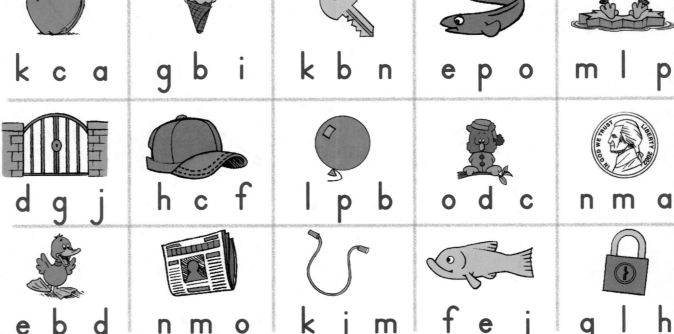

k c a   g b i   k b n   e p o   m l p

d g j   h c f   l p b   o d c   n m a

e b d   n m o   k j m   f e j   g l h

Introduction to Subtraction

Use counters (such as pennies) to make a set.
Take away the number shown. How many are left?

(Put counters here.)

Start with **5**. Take away **1**.   _____ are left.

Start with **4**. Take away **2**.   _____ are left.

Start with **7**. Take away **4**.   _____ are left.

Start with **3**. Take away **2**.   _____ is left.

The Letter Qq

queen

Trace and print.

Trace and print.

Color the pictures that start with the Qq sound.

Circle each Q and q.

Q	p	q
Q	Q	O
j	q	q

Number Match

Match the numeral to the number word.

1	five
2	six
3	two
4	ten
5	one
6	eight
7	four
8	seven
9	three
10	nine

The Letter Rr

rabbit

Trace and print.

Trace and print.

Color the pictures that start with the **R**r sound.

Circle each **R** and **r**.

How Many Are Left?

Draw an **X** to show what is taken away.
Write how many are left.

$$\begin{array}{r} 3 \\ -\ 1 \\ \hline 2 \end{array}$$

$$\begin{array}{r} 4 \\ -\ 3 \\ \hline \end{array}$$

$$\begin{array}{r} 2 \\ -\ 0 \\ \hline \end{array}$$

$$\begin{array}{r} 1 \\ -\ 1 \\ \hline \end{array}$$

$$\begin{array}{r} 3 \\ -\ 2 \\ \hline \end{array}$$

$$\begin{array}{r} 4 \\ -\ 2 \\ \hline \end{array}$$

$$\begin{array}{r} 2 \\ -\ 1 \\ \hline \end{array}$$

$$\begin{array}{r} 3 \\ -\ 3 \\ \hline \end{array}$$

$$\begin{array}{r} 4 \\ -\ 0 \\ \hline \end{array}$$

$$\begin{array}{r} 5 \\ -\ 2 \\ \hline \end{array}$$

Naming Words

Circle the naming word that names each person.

boy

girl

firefighter

zebra

baby

kitten

doctor

police officer

Too Many!

Finish the number sentence.

Think: 5 − 3 = 2

Think: 3 − =

Think: 5 − =

Think: 4 − =

Think: 4 − =

Think: 4 − =

The Letter Ss

S s

seal

Trace and print.

S S S S

Trace and print.

S S S S

Color the pictures that start with the **Ss** sound.

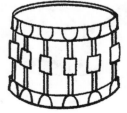

Circle each **S** and **s**.

S   G   s

e   S

s   S

s   E

My Parents and Me: Gifts to Make and Share

As parents, we strive to teach our children kindness and thoughtfulness. Making and giving gifts is one way that we can teach children to give of themselves. They will also learn about the joy of giving when they see the expression of the person who has received the gift. Here are some fun gift-making and gift-giving ideas.

Photo Greeting Cards

In today's world of technology, almost anything is possible. If you are fortunate enough to have a computer, scanner, and color printer, you and your child can create letters and greeting cards with photographs right at home. These are a real treasure! Good friends and relatives (especially grandparents) love a card made with a photograph.

Even if you do not have a computer, you can still achieve the same effect with this idea. Fold a 9" x 12" piece of construction paper in half. Cut a rectangle out of the front that is just a little bit smaller than the photo you will be using. Tape the photo behind the cutout. Decorate the front of the card. Have your child dictate a special message.

Flower Pots

Purchase some small clay flower pots. They are inexpensive and easy to decorate. Paint the pots with acrylics and then spray with shellac. Glue buttons, ricrac, sequins, glitter, ribbons, and other decorations on the pots. Almost anything can be glued or painted on a clay pot.

You will be surprised at how darling the clay pots are when they are finished. For extra fun, have your child plant a flower in the pot for the perfect gift!

Notepads

Simple notepads can be created using a variety of materials. The firm back of the notepad can be made from thick cardboard, plywood, plastic, or even tile. Let your child decorate whatever material you have chosen for the back. (See illustration.) Cut sheets of paper smaller than the back so the recipient of the gift can see the designs your child has created. Attach the paper with a clothespin. Paint the clothespin to match.

Butterfly Pins and Magnets

Purchase some miniature clothespins (found at most craft stores). Let your child paint the clothespins and allow them to dry. Add facial features to the butterfly with a black fine-tip permanent marker. Create wings with colored tissue paper. (See illustration.) Add a strip of self-adhesive magnetic tape to the back to make a magnet, or use hot glue to attach a safety pin (an adult should do this).

Fabric Painting

See "Fabric Painting" on page 65 for additional gift ideas.

The Letter Tt

turtle

Trace and print.

Trace and print.

Color the pictures that start with the Tt sound.

Circle each T and t.

Story Problem Subtraction

Write a number sentence to solve each problem.

4 birds sat in a tree.
2 flew away.
Now there are _2_ birds.

4 − 2 = 2

4 bees sat on a flower.
1 bee flew away.
How many bees were left?

___ − ___ = ___

3 balloons float in the air.
1 balloon pops.
Now there are _____ balloons left.

___ − ___ = ___

5 ducks swam in the pond.
3 ducks flew away.
How many were left?

___ − ___ = ___

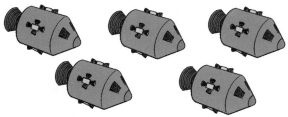

5 rockets flew to the moon.
2 rockets came home.
How many stayed on the moon?

___ − ___ = ___

3 prairie dogs popped up.
2 prairie dogs went back down.
How many are still up?

___ − ___ = ___

The Letter Uu

umbrella

Trace and print.

Trace and print.

Circle the pictures that have the **short Uu** sound. Draw an **X** on the pictures with the **long Uu** sound.

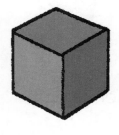

Numbers to 50

Fill in the missing numbers.

1 ___ ___ 4 ___

___ 7 ___ ___ 10

___ ___ 13 ___ ___

16 ___ 18 ___ 20

___ 22 ___ ___ 25

26 ___ ___ 29 ___

___ 32 ___ ___ 35

___ ___ 38 ___ ___

41 ___ ___ 44 ___

___ 47 ___ ___ 50

The Letter Vv

valentine

Trace and print.

Trace and print.

Color the pictures that start with the Vv sound.

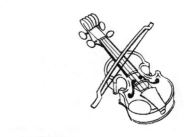

Circle each V and v.

V   v

v

u   V   v

W   V   U

Which Sign?

Read the stories and answer the questions.
Write a number sentence to show each answer.
Do not forget to write the **+** or **−** in the circle.

A.   Together, Steve and Peter planted **9** rows of carrots.
Peter planted **3** rows.
How many rows did Steve plant?

_____   _____ = _____

B.   Kim and Mary picked **7** flowers altogether.
Mary picked **3** flowers.
How many flowers did Kim pick?

_____   _____ = _____

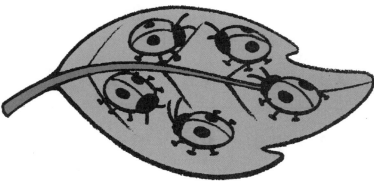

C.   There were **5** ladybugs on a leaf.
Later, **2** more ladybugs flew to the leaf.
How many ladybugs were there in all?

_____   _____ = _____

Counting to 100

Practice counting to 100.

1	2	3	4	5	6	7	8	9	10
11	12	13	14	15	16	17	18	19	20
21	22	23	24	25	26	27	28	29	30
31	32	33	34	35	36	37	38	39	40
41	42	43	44	45	46	47	48	49	50
51	52	53	54	55	56	57	58	59	60
61	62	63	64	65	66	67	68	69	70
71	72	73	74	75	76	77	78	79	80
81	82	83	84	85	86	87	88	89	90
91	92	93	94	95	96	97	98	99	100

1. String 100 pieces of cereal on a piece of string.

2. Write the numerals 1 to 100 on a piece of adding machine tape. How long is the paper? Ask an adult to help you measure the paper.

Letter Review S-V

Circle the correct beginning sound.

s   t   v

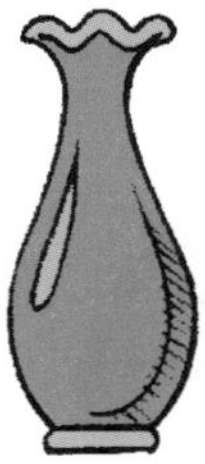

u   s   v

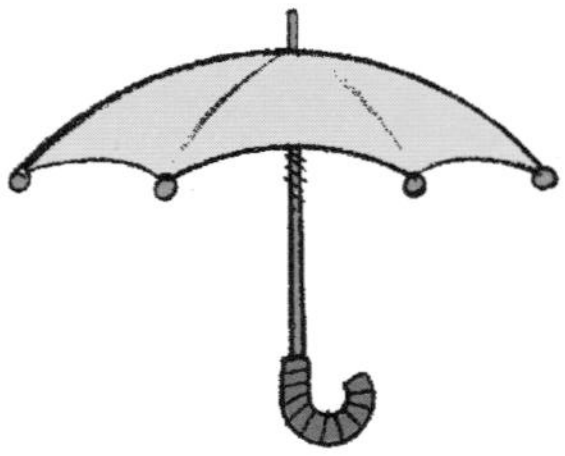

t   v   u

t   s   u

v   u   t

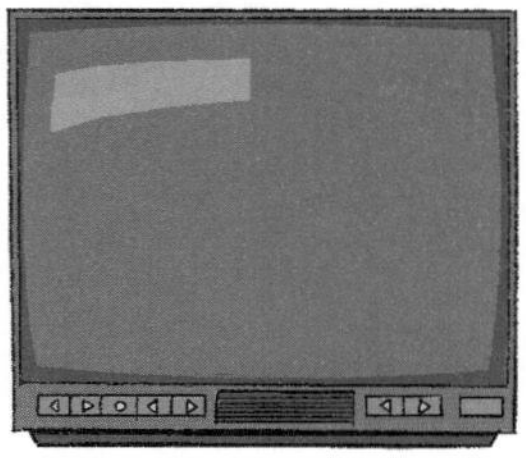

t   u   s

u   v   s

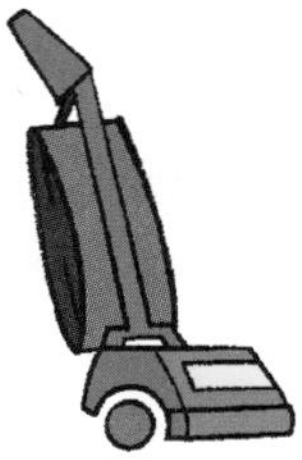

s   v   t

Time on the Hour

Write the time you see on each clock.

A.

6:00

B.

___:___

C.

___:___

D.

___:___

E.

___:___

F.

___:___

G.

___:___

H.

___:___

The Letter Ww

walrus

Trace and print.

Trace and print.

Color the pictures that start with the **Ww** sound.

Circle each **W** and **w**.

W   V   w
W   W   V
W   M   w
          w

Half and Whole

Trace and color the **whole** picture.

Trace and color **half** of each picture.

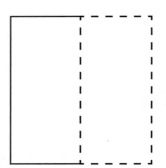

Color the **whole** pictures **red**. Color the **half** pictures **blue**.

The Letter Xx

X ray

Trace and print.

Trace and print.

Color the pictures that start with the Xx sound.

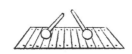

Circle each X and x.

Subtraction to 10

Count up to subtract. Write the difference.
Use the code to color the picture.

Color Code

2 = blue
3 = red
4 = green
5 = yellow
6 = black
7 = orange
8 = pink
9 = purple

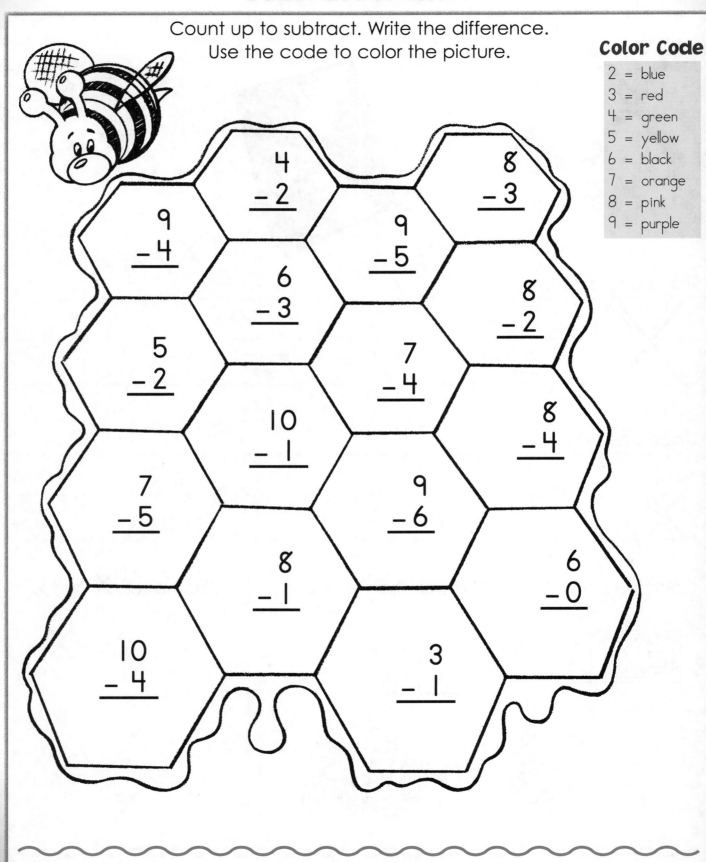

The Letter Yy

yo-yo

Trace and print.

Trace and print.

Color the pictures that start with the Yy sound.

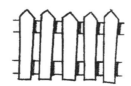

Circle each Y and y.

Fact Families

Did you know that numbers have families, too?
Write the missing numerals in each family.

A. Family: **6, 2, 8**

$6 + \boxed{} = 8$

$2 + 6 = \boxed{}$

$8 - \boxed{} = 2$

$8 - 2 = \boxed{}$

B. Family: **10, 7, 3**

$7 + \boxed{} = 10$

$3 + 7 = \boxed{}$

$10 - 7 = \boxed{}$

$10 - \boxed{} = 7$

C. Family: **5, 3, 2**

$3 + 2 = \boxed{}$

$2 + \boxed{} = 5$

$5 - 3 = \boxed{}$

$5 - \boxed{} = 3$

D. Family: **4, 3, 1**

$3 + \boxed{} = 4$

$\boxed{} + 3 = \boxed{}$

$4 - \boxed{} = 3$

$4 - \boxed{} = 1$

The Letter Zz

Zz

zebra

Trace and print.

Trace and print.

Color the pictures that start with the Zz sound.

Circle each Z and z.

Z   w   z

z   z   s

Z   S   Z

Subtraction Assessment

Find the difference.

$$\begin{array}{r} 1 \\ -\ 1 \\ \hline \end{array}$$
$$\begin{array}{r} 8 \\ -\ 3 \\ \hline \end{array}$$
$$\begin{array}{r} 5 \\ -\ 3 \\ \hline \end{array}$$
$$\begin{array}{r} 7 \\ -\ 0 \\ \hline \end{array}$$

$$\begin{array}{r} 9 \\ -\ 2 \\ \hline \end{array}$$
$$\begin{array}{r} 6 \\ -\ 3 \\ \hline \end{array}$$
$$\begin{array}{r} 8 \\ -\ 4 \\ \hline \end{array}$$
$$\begin{array}{r} 7 \\ -\ 5 \\ \hline \end{array}$$

$$\begin{array}{r} 10 \\ -\ 5 \\ \hline \end{array}$$
$$\begin{array}{r} 5 \\ -\ 1 \\ \hline \end{array}$$
$$\begin{array}{r} 9 \\ -\ 4 \\ \hline \end{array}$$
$$\begin{array}{r} 2 \\ -\ 1 \\ \hline \end{array}$$

$$\begin{array}{r} 4 \\ -\ 0 \\ \hline \end{array}$$
$$\begin{array}{r} 3 \\ -\ 2 \\ \hline \end{array}$$
$$\begin{array}{r} 3 \\ -\ 3 \\ \hline \end{array}$$
$$\begin{array}{r} 6 \\ -\ 2 \\ \hline \end{array}$$

Remove pages 147–150. Cut along dashed lines. Staple pages in order.

ALPHABET SOUNDS

A "Matching" Book

Draw a line to match each picture with its beginning sound.

Hh

Jj

Kk

Ll

Mm

Draw a line to match each picture with its beginning sound.

Bb

Cc

Dd

Ff

Gg

Draw a line to match each picture with its beginning sound.

Nn

Pp

Qq

Rr

Ss

Draw a line to match each picture with its beginning sound.

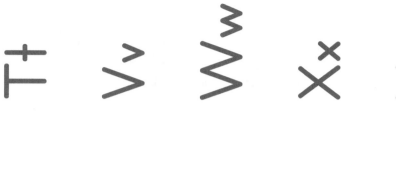

Tt

Vv

Ww

Xx

Yy

Zz

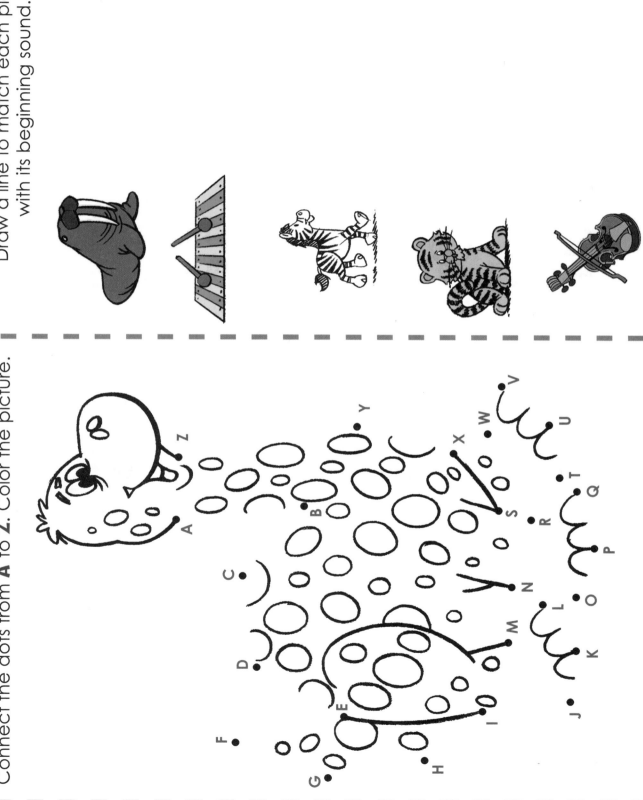

Connect the dots from **A** to **Z**. Color the picture.

149

Draw a line to match each picture with its beginning sound.

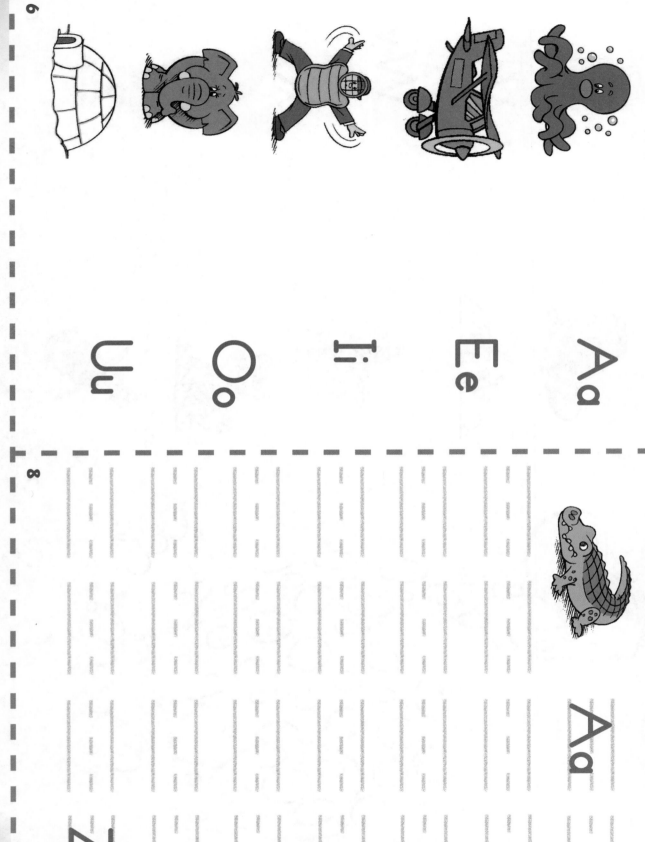

Uu

Oo

Ii

Ee

Aa

Print the alphabet with **uppercase** and **lowercase** letters.

Aa

Zz

Alphabet Assessment

Circle the correct beginning sound.

B S T		I O L		C B J		Y X W	
T B K		C A G		M N O		C G D	
U R B		F R T		S R T		M N O	
C T Q		Y X Z		P T J		E D C	
H F E		J W V		M P O		T Q R	
U T V		Q P O		U X V		E F G	
J I P		Y X Z				correct / 26 total	

151

Sight Word Activities

Sight words are words that your child is not expected to be able to sound out phonically. They are common words that children often learn to read simply by remembering what the words look like. Although your child may not be sounding out words until he is in first grade, sight words can provide young children with the "experience" of beginning to read. Pages 153–157 contain 32 different sight word cards. Below are some suggestions for using the words in games and activities to help your child begin to read.

Sight Word Games

Make a photocopy of each of the flash card pages before cutting. Cover the cards in laminate or clear contact paper for durability and then cut them apart. With two sets of cards, your child will be able to play memory and match games. Children must be able to see the similarities and differences in the cards before they will be able to recognize and remember the words. Give your child lots of experience in matching the cards. Match two that are the same and tell your child what the cards say.

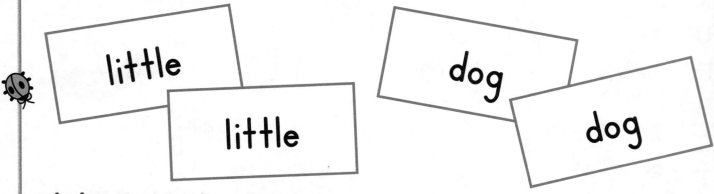

Printing the Words

Provide your child with the experience of printing the words with finger paint or in salt, sand, or even mud. The multisensory experience will help your child remember the word when he or she is able to "see it," "feel it," and "say it."

Making Phrases and Sentences

Learning to read a phrase or sentence is a thrilling experience for a young child. Begin with a small phrase, such as "Run dog." Have your child print the phrase at the bottom of a piece of paper, then create an illustration to accompany the phrase. You will be surprised to see how many sentences (and stories) you can create using only 32 words. Here are some sample sentences to get you going.

I see you.	The cat can play with me.	See the little dog jump.
Can you run?	I like the big red cat.	Can you see me?
Do you like to play?	Look at the little dog.	Dog and cat come here!
I am here.	You are one funny dog!	I can play with you.
It is my cat.	Come and run with me.	I am here to look at the dog.

a	I	am
come		see
me		you
the		and
here		my

it	is	like
cat		dog
big		little
one		can
look		jump

funny	play
run	with
at	not
red	do
to	have

Cut-and-Color Awards

Parent: Have your child decorate and color these awards. Fill in your child's name and the date to mark each accomplishment. The awards can be worn as badges or put into small frames.

I know my beginning consonant sounds!

Name: _____ Date: _____

I can read number words!

Name: _____ Date: _____

I can read color words!

Name: _____ Date: _____

I can tell time on the hour!

Name: _____ Date: _____

I can count to 50!

Name: _____ Date: _____

I can add with counters!

Name: _____ Date: _____

I can name all the shapes!

Name: _____ Date: _____

I can subtract with counters!

Name: _____ Date: _____